teach®
yourself

home PC maintenance
and networking

®
teach yourself

home PC maintenance and networking

anthony price

For UK order enquiries: please contact Bookpoint Ltd, 130 Milton Park, Abingdon, Oxon OX14 4SB. Telephone: +44 (0)1235 827720. Fax: +44 (0)1235 400454. Lines are open 09.00–17.00, Monday to Saturday, with a 24-hour message answering service. Details about our titles and how to order are available at www.teachyourself.co.uk.

For USA order enquiries: please contact McGraw-Hill Customer Services, PO Box 545, Blacklick, OH 43004-0545, USA. Telephone: 1-800-722-4726. Fax: 1-614-755-5645.

For Canada order enquiries: please contact McGraw-Hill Ryerson Ltd, 300 Water St, Whitby, Ontario L1N 9B6, Canada. Telephone: 905 430 5000. Fax: 905 430 5020.

Long renowned as the authoritative source for self-guided learning – with more than 50 million copies sold worldwide – the **teach yourself** series includes over 500 titles in the fields of languages, crafts, hobbies, business, computing and education.

British Library Cataloguing in Publication Data: a catalogue record for this title is available from The British Library.

Library of Congress Catalog Card Number: on file.

First published in UK 2006 by Hodder Education, 338 Euston Road, London NW1 3BH.

First published in US 2006 by The McGraw-Hill Companies, Inc.

The **teach yourself** name is a registered trademark of Hodder Headline.

Computer hardware and software brand names mentioned in this book are protected by their respective trademarks and are acknowledged.

Copyright © 2006 Anthony Price

Typeset by MacDesign, Southampton

Printed in Great Britain for Hodder Education, a division of Hodder Headline, 338 Euston Road, London NW1 3BH, by Cox & Wyman Ltd, Reading, Berkshire.

The publisher has used its best endeavours to ensure that the URLs for external websites referred to in this book are co©rrect and active at the time of going to press. However, the publisher and the author have no responsibility for the websites and can make no guarantee that a site will remain live or that the content will remain relevant, decent or appropriate.

Hodder Headline's policy is to use papers that are natural, renewable and recyclable products and made from wood grown in sustainable forests. The logging and manufacturing processes are expected to conform to the environmental regulations of the country of origin.

Impression number   10 9 8 7 6 5 4 3 2 1

Year   2010 2009 2008 2007 2006

contents

This book is about the basics: the jobs you can do yourself on your PC with a bit of know-how and a screwdriver. If you can use a computer as an everyday tool for word processing, email, etc. there are many jobs that you can handle. With the aid of *Teach Yourself Home PC Maintenance and Networking*, you can:

* Maintain the system at peak efficiency.

* Manage anti-virus and security measures.

* Upgrade or add hard disks, CD and DVD drives or RAM.

* Replace a dead power supply unit.

* Diagnose software and hardware faults.

* Attach peripheral devices, e.g. a printer, scanner or camera, to the standard external ports.

* Set up and manage a home network to share an Internet connection and/or a printer or scanner.

Even where you decide that a job is too big for you – and you'll be surprised at what you can do for yourself if you're willing to have a go – you will be able to:

* Make a support phone call clearly and with confidence.

* Discuss problems with a professional technical support worker in the language that *they* understand.

* Be sure that work proposed for your system is necessary.

* Check that all work is carried out effectively.

Teach Yourself Home PC Maintenance and Networking is not intended to turn you into a qualified PC technician: there are other books and courses which aim to do that. What it *will* do is save you money on your PC maintenance bills by putting *you* in control of *your* system. You will find that most PC maintenance is easy enough (when you know how) and once you have done a few jobs for yourself you may even find that you enjoy it!

The structure of the book

This book is divided into three sections: *The operating system*, *hardware* and *basic networking*.

The operating system

The operating system is the software that makes the computer 'go': without operating system software a PC is simply a collection of components. The Windows operating system has evolved through several releases, and a small book cannot cover them all in detail. The differences between the modern Windows versions – the various flavours of XP and Vista – are not particularly important for most of the tasks outlined in the text. Where differences *are* significant they are noted in the text.

This book does not aim to teach you Windows – there are many books such as *Teach Yourself Windows XP* or *Teach Yourself Windows Vista* which aim to do that. This book assumes that you are familiar with the basics of pointing and clicking with a mouse and entering text from a keyboard.

Many, if not most, of the common problems that users encounter from time to time have their causes and solutions in the Windows operating system. For example, defragmenting a disk drive requires half a dozen mouse clicks to set it going; it completes in a few minutes and usually makes a noticeable difference to system performance. Chapter 1 will show you how and why you should do this, along with some other easy and useful tasks.

You can enhance the performance of Windows by selectively adding and removing Windows components and third-party applications through the *Control Panel*, and you can choose your start-up options with the system configurations utility *msconfig*.

At some stage in the life of a PC you may need to reinstall the operating system. This may be through a manufacturer's Restore CD/DVD or a conventional installation from a Windows XP CD or Vista DVD. Both methods are described in Chapter 13, *Installing/reinstalling Windows*.

xi
preface

Hardware

Modern hardware is generally robust and reliable but it still needs to be replaced or upgraded from time to time. There are some components, such as system RAM and expansion cards for (say) networking which can be easily installed in a few minutes by anyone with a screwdriver and a brain. Chapter 8, *Replacing and upgrading hardware* takes you through what you need to know to do these upgrades. It also shows you how to fit a second hard disk on your system and how to configure it and use it for storage.

Other hardware components, such as the CPU chip or the motherboard are less likely to be on the agenda for most home users. Changing a motherboard or a CPU is a non-trivial undertaking: above all it is not often cost-effective. Fitting (say) a 20% faster CPU will not deliver a 20% increase in system performance. This book will equip you to analyse and discuss such hardware upgrades with confidence.

Basic networking

There's a world of difference between the sort of large network that many of us encounter in the workplace, and the needs of the home or small office user. In the multi-user workplace environment there are often complex security issues: who can log in where and when, and what resources they may use. Fortunately, for most of us, there is usually a technical support team to deal with them. For the home or small office user, *Teach Yourself Home PC Maintenance and Networking* will take you step-by-step through what is needed by most of us:

◆ Setting up a basic peer-to-peer Local Area Network (LAN) – from 2 to 5 PCs linked by cabling or wireless technologies.

◆ Setting up and sharing an Internet connection across your LAN using an ADSL modem, a conventional dialup modem, or a broadband router which combines Internet access and local networking capabilities.

◆ Your home/small office network may not need all the security and access controls of the one at work, but you will need to take some common sense precautions against intrusions and malicious programs: viruses, trojans, spyware, etc. Chapters 15–17 look at security issues that will affect the home user.

About you

You have a PC and you are comfortable using it. You know how to manage your files, and how to use the Internet and email. You have occasional PC problems which you sometimes find annoying, but you don't like the prices charged by PC technicians for a call-out. Neither do you want the trouble of disconnecting everything, bundling it into the car and taking it to a workshop or repair centre and still paying for a job that you suspect that you might be able to do yourself if only you knew how.

Maybe you have more than one PC, or you want to be able to share files between your laptop and your desktop or office PC through a home network. Or you may just be curious – wanting to know how your PC works rather than simply how to work it.

If you can change a light bulb, mend a fuse, or check the oil in your car, you can do most of the jobs necessary to keep your PC working, and working well. All you need is a basic book (this one), a screwdriver and the willingness to have a go, to experiment – to teach yourself.

Acknowledgements

Thanks are due to Tracey Williams for reading the original typescript with the eye of an A+ qualified working PC technician, for checking the examples and for correcting a number of errors. Any errors which remain are entirely my responsibility.

Anthony Price
2006

About the author

Anthony Price is an experienced teacher and field engineer. He has over 20 years' experience in the technical aspects of PCs, teaches computer maintenance at an Adult Education College and has written a book aimed at professional PC technicians: *A+ for Students* (Hodder Arnold). He holds a Master of Science degree in Information Technology and is a working director of a PC maintenance company.

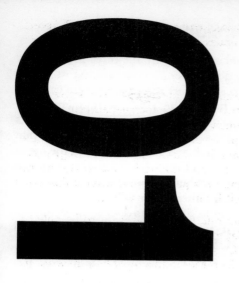

01

maintaining Windows

In this chapter you will learn:

- how to tell which version of Windows you are running

- four maintenance things you can do now

- about the Administrator account

- how to use Safe Mode

1.1 Windows versions

XP Home, XP Professional and Vista are the three most widely used versions of the Windows operating system. Most of the time, the differences between them are not important for carrying out system maintenance tasks. The Disk Defragmenter, for example, is almost identical in all three versions, though its appearance across them varies. Another minor variation is that XP systems have separate Search and Run features on the menu to the right of the Start button, whereas Vista has a Start Search box immediately above the Start button. From here you can start a search of your PC, or of the Internet, or launch a program by typing its name. For example, if you have Microsoft Office installed, typing 'Winword' in the Vista Start Search box will launch the word processor, Word.

Other differences will be noted where necessary in the text. For example, Vista uses the terms *Computer* and *Documents* where XP (Home and Professional) uses the terms *My Computer* and *My Documents* for the corresponding items. Occasionally, there are more fundamental differences and these will be explained as necessary. For example, accessing the *Administrator* user account is done differently in the Home edition of XP.

One of the similarities across the different Windows versions is the ability to set the system up to respond to single or double left mouse clicks to open a file or run a program. If your machine is set up for 'double-click' – the default value – when you see 'click' in the text just read it as 'double-click'.

In general, all of the Windows versions are highly configurable. Windows XP when set for 'best performance' looks very like the older Windows 2000. Vista – unless it is running on top whack hardware – may well look very like XP. The good news is that these settings are under your control.

To find which version of Windows you are using, and other information about your system, right-click on the *(My) Computer* icon and select *Properties*. You will see something similar to Figure 1.01a. This shows the *Properties* of a fairly old machine (a PIII) running the Home edition of Windows XP with Service Pack 2 installed. It is unlikely that you will be using a machine

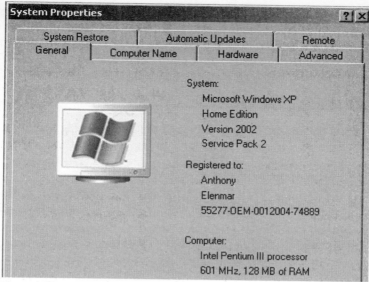

Figure 1.01a

which doesn't have this Service Pack, but if you are, obtaining it and installing it is a straightforward job. Chapter 13, *Installing/ reinstalling Windows* shows how this is done.

At the other end of the hardware scale, Figure 1.01b shows a more modern PC running Vista.

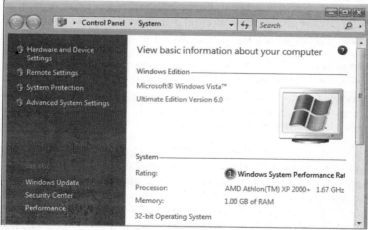

Figure 1.01b

At first sight, this is rather different from the XP version, but the method of reaching this panel is the same and the information presented is similar. For much of the time, you will find that your XP knowledge will adapt quite easily to the parts of Vista that concern us for maintenance purposes.

XP Home

This is the consumer-level release of the XP operating system. It is designed for ease of use and lacks some features of the Professional product. It is often pre-installed on systems bought from High Street or Internet retailers.

XP Home does not support more than one CPU processor, it cannot join a domain-based network and has a limit of five machines on a peer-to-peer home network. The *Backup* utility is not installed by default (as it is in the Professional version) but it can be installed from the original XP installation CD if required. For most home or home office users these restrictions don't cause any problems.

XP Professional

XP Professional does not have the restrictions of the Home edition and, as you might expect, it costs more to buy. In day-to-day use you will barely notice the difference on a home or home office machine. For some tasks, however, the Professional version of XP is easier to use. For example, it is easier to use the built-in *Administrator* user account in Professional than in Home, and security settings are more easily accessible. Where these differences are important they are noted in the text.

Vista

Vista is the latest version of Windows. It is the biggest and most sophisticated to date. It has been designed to have much of the look and feel of XP, albeit with some extra features. However, for most of the maintenance tasks that you will want to carry out, it is fundamentally similar in operation and appearance to earlier Windows versions.

Vista has all the capabilities of XP Professional and more. It is however, a big and resource-hungry piece of software. Microsoft recommends a minimum of 15gigabytes of disk space just for Vista, and the required 512Mb of RAM is unlikely to be sufficient for anything but light use. It is possible to upgrade an XP machine to run Vista, but you may run into hardware compatibility problems which are beyond the scope of this book.

1.2 Four things you can do now

PC systems tend to slow down through time for various reasons. Moreover, they are often set up to give the most attractive appearance at the expense of performance, and this can be significant if you have an older or relatively low-powered PC.

Before you start, consider the safety and integrity of your data. The tools you are about to use are safe and reliable and have been in use by millions of users for many years. However, things *do* go wrong very occasionally. For example, a mains power failure part way through a disk defragmentation could cause data loss or corruption.

As a rule, it is wise to back up data and make a note of settings before doing any maintenance work. See Chapter 6, *Backup strategies* for more information on this. Having backed up your data (or decided to accept the small risk of not doing so) we can get down to business with the operating system tools.

Note: some of the utilities on some systems may require you to have Administrator rights to use them. If, when you try to access a utility, you receive an error message along the lines of 'You do not have sufficient rights to …' You may have to log in as the Administrator user in order to work with them. Using the Administrator account is described later in this chapter.

Check Disk

Like many Windows utilities, Check Disk can be accessed through several routes. Space limitations mean that it is not possible to describe them all here. Perhaps the easiest way is to select the disk you wish to check, then select from the Tools menu. To run Check Disk:

1   Click (or double-click) on **My Computer**.

2 Right-click on the C: drive and select **Properties**.

3 Select the **Tools** tab.

4 Click **Check Now**.

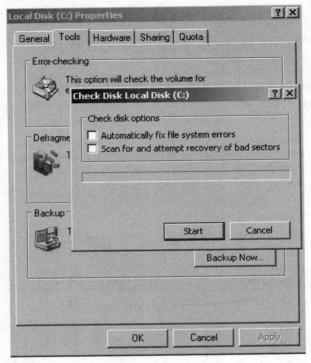

Figure 1.02

Figure 1.02 shows the Check Disk utility in XP. Click **Start** to begin. If you leave the two option boxes unchecked (the default value), Check Disk will simply check the file system for errors. More thorough testing can be done by selecting either or both of the check boxes. Depending on the choice you make, you may have to restart the machine. If you do this, the disk will be checked as the PC starts up and you will see a (probably unfamiliar) text-based screen – white characters on a blue screen – which will report progress and, when complete, continue the boot process to the usual Desktop.

The Disk Cleanup Wizard

Hard disks accumulate rubbish files through time – temporary files from application installers and the Internet are probably the worst culprits. These files take up disk space and, especially if the disk is fairly full, can slow the system down substantially. The Disk Cleanup Wizard is the Windows utility to deal with these unwanted files and it is available in all Windows versions.

1 Click on **My Computer**.

2 Right-click on the C: drive and select **Properties**.

3 Select the **General** tab.

4 Click **Disk Cleanup**.

The system will spend a few seconds gathering information and will then present you with some options.

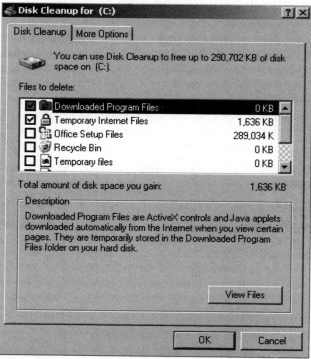

Figure 1.03 The Cleanup options in XP Professional

5 Accept the default values, or change them by checking or unchecking boxes.

6 When you have made your choices click **OK**. You will be asked 'Are you sure you want to perform these actions?' – Click the **Yes** button if you do.

The system will then display its progress and offer the option to cancel until it is finished.

The Disk Defragmenter

Imagine a library where returned books are placed on the first available shelf space and the catalogue is updated to record their new position. After a while, books would be shelved all over the place, and something like a multi-volume encyclopedia would take a long time to find because the individual volumes would be on different shelves or even different floors of the building.

Windows stores files rather like the books in the library example. When a file is written to the hard disk it is written to the first available storage unit (cluster). A large file may be written across several clusters and these may be widely separated. When files are deleted it makes more clusters available, possibly in the middle of other files. This is known as *fragmentation* and the answer to the problem is *defragmentation*: that is, rearranging the storage clusters so that all parts of the same file are on the same part of the hard disk, making them easier to find and quicker to load.

To use the Defragmentation utility:

1 In (My) Computer, right-click on the C: drive and select **Properties** then the **Tools** tab.

2 Click **Defragment Now**.

3 You will be given the option to defragment the volume or analyse it. Choosing **Analyse** will indicate the level of fragmentation on the disk and the system will recommend (or not) that you defrag the disk. Even where Windows doesn't recommend that you defrag, you can go ahead and do it anyway, if you want to – just click **Defragment**.

Figure 1.04 shows the report from XP indicating the level of fragmentation. The information is colour coded (not visible in the figure): white represents *free space*, blue shows *contiguous* (non-fragmented) *files*, red indicates *fragmented files* and the green shows *unmovable files* – these are typically protected operating system files such as the Master File Table which is the 'index' of the files on the disk.

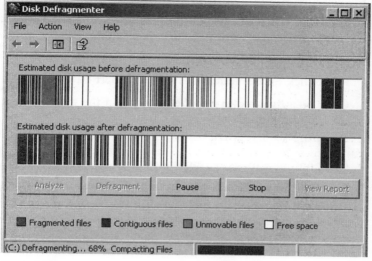

Figure 1.04

Defragging a large disk can be a long process, particularly if it hasn't been done for a while. You can continue working while it runs, but this will slow the process down even further. If you defragged a week ago, set it running and make some coffee. If it has been a couple of months since your last defrag there will probably be time for a three-course meal! It is however, worth doing from time to time.

System Settings Visual Effects tab

XP/Vista are both designed to be visually attractive, with 3-D buttons, sliding or fading menus and other visual effects. If you like these features and you have a reasonably powerful machine to support them, fine. However, if you want to release some processing power you can modify these special effects through the XP/Vista interface.

To change the settings in XP:

1 Right-click on **My Computer** and select **Properties**.

2 Choose the **Advanced** tab.

3 Click the **Settings** button under **Performance**.

4 Select the **Visual Effects** tab. From here you can select which visual effects you want to enable or disable.

To change the settings in Vista:

1 Right-click on **Computer** and select **Properties**.

2 Click on **Advanced System Settings** (from the menu bar on the left of the display).

3 Select the **Advanced** tab.

4 Click on the **Settings** button under **Performance**.

5 Select the **Visual Effects** tab. From here you can select which visual effects you want to enable or disable.

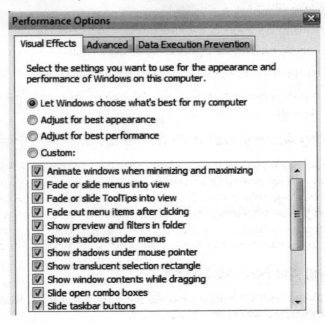

Figure 1.05

Figure 1.05 shows the Visual Effects settings in Vista. They are set to the default value of 'Let Windows choose' and in this instance it has chosen settings which are the same as the Best Appearance settings. Selecting Best Performance will disable all of the visual effects. Custom settings allows you to choose the combination of visual effects that you want by checking or unchecking the appropriate boxes. The range of choices varies somewhat between Windows versions and the best way to decide what you want is simply to experiment. If you don't like the results, you can always change them back!

1.3 Using the Administrator account

All Windows versions have a special user account called *Administrator* which has the rights to do anything on the system. (See Chapter 13, *Installing/reinstalling Windows* for more on this.) It is often necessary to have Administrator rights in order to carry out a task such as changing the system time and date, or installing/uninstalling software.

There are three ways to obtain Administrator rights.

- Give Administrator rights to an ordinary user.
- Use the Run As option (not available in XP Home).
- Log on to the system with the Administrator user name and password.

Giving Administrator rights to an ordinary user

This is how Windows is set up by default on most systems. When the operating system is installed, an Administrator account is created along with a standard user account, usually in the name of the person who owns the machine. This first user account is a member of a user group called Administrators (in the plural) and the user account has *most* of the rights of the Administrator.

Using the Run As option

Both Vista and XP Professional edition have a facility to Run As Administrator where this is necessary.

1 Right-click on the icon of the program you want to run.

2 Select **Run As** from the context menu. This will display the Run As dialog box.

Figure 1.06 shows the user 'Anthony' on an XP professional machine. The User name field is a drop-down list of all users on the machine, with the Administrator as the default value at the top of the list. In order to run the program, the user types in the Administrator password and the program will run just as if he or she were using the Administrator account.

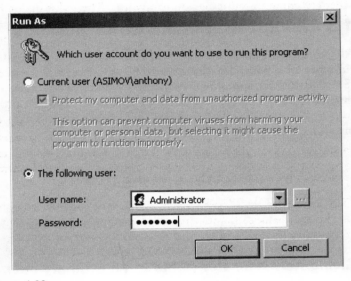

Figure 1.06

The Home edition of XP has the Run As facility, but the Administrator account cannot be accessed through it. By default, users on XP Home have Administrator rights, but where these are not sufficient for the task in hand it is necessary to log on using the Administrator account.

In Vista, the Run facility is presented slightly differently but, as with many of the differences between Windows versions, this is more a matter of appearance than of substance.

Logging on as Administrator

Logging on as Administrator is often a requirement for uninstalling a program, even where it may have been originally installed using the Run As option or even by a standard user with Administrator rights. It is also a good idea to log on as Administrator when you have several tasks to perform rather than repeatedly using Run As.

XP Home, XP Professional and Vista can all be set up to require users to log on through a standard dialog box which requires them to enter a user name and password. Where this dialog box is not displayed, but you see a Welcome screen instead, press [Control], [Alt] and [Delete] simultaneously, twice, and the logon dialog box will then be displayed. On XP Professional and Vista systems you can simply type in the user name Administrator and the appropriate password.

Where you have a machine set up for a single user with no password the system skips past the Welcome screen almost too quickly to see it. The solution is to wait until the machine reaches a stable Desktop then choose the Log Off option. This will take you to the Welcome screen where you can use the [Control], [Alt] and [Delete] combination as described above.

This will work on a Home machine, too, but there is little point in doing it because the user name ADMINISTRATOR won't be recognized. The only way to access the Administrator account on an XP Home machine is by booting into Safe Mode.

1.4 Using Safe Mode

Safe Mode is a special diagnostic mode of Windows operation. It loads and runs the operating system with the minimum of drivers, so you have no sound capabilities and only a fairly primitive graphics display. It is sometimes possible to boot to Safe Mode when a machine won't otherwise start. For example, if display settings are wrong and the screen is unreadable in normal operation, you can use Safe Mode to correct the problem.

1   Boot to Safe Mode to change the display settings.

2   In XP, right-click on an empty area of the Desktop, select the **Settings** tab and make the necessary adjustments.

3   In Vista, right-click on an empty area of the Desktop, select the **Personalize** option from the context menu, then choose **Display Settings**.

On either version of Windows you can now make the necessary adjustments, then reboot the machine into normal mode.

- To access Safe Mode, hold down [F8] as the machine boots. You will be presented with a menu which includes Safe Mode as one of the options. Use the arrow keys to navigate to the option you require and press [Enter] to confirm your choice.

- In XP Home edition, booting to Safe Mode will present you with an option to use System Restore to take the system back to a previous state. System Restore is available in all Windows versions and is covered in Chapter 2, *System Tools*.

Summary

This chapter has introduced the three most widely used Windows versions and has outlined the main differences between them from a system maintenance point of view.

You have been introduced to some maintenance tools: Check Disk, Disk Cleanup and Defrag, and shown how to change the look of Windows to improve performance.

The Administrator user account has been outlined in the context of permissions needed to carry out some maintenance tasks.

You will have observed, that even while the appearance and details vary between the different Windows versions, the tools and techniques remain fundamentally similar. Using some, or all, of them can produce noticeable improvements in the performance of your system.

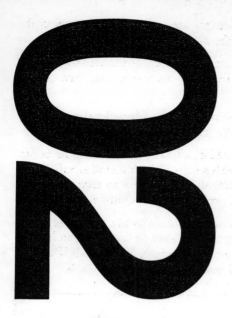

02

system tools

In this chapter you will learn:

- about activating Windows

- how to use the System Tools

- how to access System Information

- about the Files and Settings Transfer Wizard

2.1 System Tools

All Windows versions provide several System Tools. To see what is available on your system:

• Click **Start,** point to **All Programs** then **Accessories** and select **System Tools.**

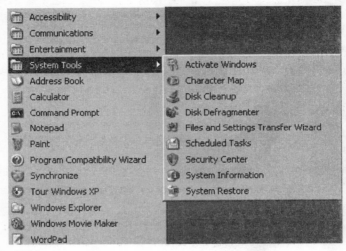

Figure 2.01

Figure 2.01 shows the System Tools on an XP Home system. Note that there is no entry for Backup: users of this edition need to install this manually (more below). Two entries will be familiar: we have already seen Disk Cleanup and Disk Defragmenter though we accessed them by a different route earlier.

In Windows there is often more than one way of doing something. For example, many of the System Tools can also be accessed through the Control Panel (see Chapter 3).

Activate Windows

Unless you have only just installed Windows you can ignore this. As an anti-piracy feature Windows requires that you activate it within 30 days of installation. This only has to be done once after installing (or reinstalling) Windows. This topic is addressed in Chapter 13.

Backup

The Backup utility is part of all Windows versions, though there are differences between them. Vista, in particular, has more features than XP. Home and Professional versions of XP use the same pre-Vista version of Backup but it is not installed by default in the Home edition. If you are using XP Home and you want to use Backup you will need to install it first. If you are using XP Professional skip to section 2.2, or if you have Vista skip to 2.3.

Note: for many users the Windows Backup utility may not be the best option. Chapter 6, *Backup strategies*, looks at some alternatives.

Installing Backup in XP Home

The Backup utility in XP Home has to be installed from the installation CD. Here's how.

1 Put the installation CD into the drive and either hold down [Shift] to prevent it from auto-running or simply close the Welcome window by clicking on Exit.

2 Next, go to My Computer and right-click on the icon for the CD drive and select Explore from the context menu.

3 Use Windows Explorer to navigate to your CDROM drive and select the folder:

D:VALUEADD\MSFT\NTBACKUP

The left pane of Figure 2.02 shows the path through the folder structure on the CD. The right pane shows the contents; in this case a Readme file and an installer for the Backup utility called NTBACKUP.MSI.

4 Click on this file's icon to install the Backup utility.

5 When the installer has finished – a couple of seconds – navigate to the *System Tools* menu and you will see that the *Backup* utility has been tacked on to the end of the menu.

With *Backup* installed the Home and Professional versions of XP are the same.

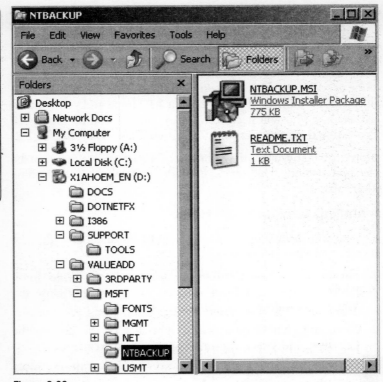

Figure 2.02

2.2 XP Backup

When you click on Backup in the System Tools menu you will be presented with the Welcome screen shown in Figure 2.03. (The default is to start in Wizard mode – accept this. Advanced mode gives us more features, but at the expense of some – for most users – unnecessary complexity.)

Clicking **Next** will present you with another screen which asks you to choose between a Backup and a Restore operation. For this exercise choose the default – Backup. Click **Next**.

You will be presented with four choices of files to back up:

* *My Documents and Settings* refers to the documents and settings of the current user.

Figure 2.03

- *Everyone's Documents and Settings* refers to all users of the PC.

- The *All Information on This Computer* option is, to put it bluntly, a waste of time. If you want to back up everything there are better methods than MS Backup – third-party utilities such as *Norton Ghost* will do the job better and more easily.

- *Let Me Choose What to Backup* takes you to a dialogue which allows you to choose the files to be included in a backup job. Figure 2.04 illustrates this.

The selection in the figure is to back up documents and settings for the user 'Anthony'. To select any set of files or folders to back up, simply check the box next to them. This applies to files and folders on the local machine as well as any other machines visible on the network (if you have one).

Regardless of what you have chosen to include in your backup job, the next step is to decide *where* to back up. By default, the Backup utility will suggest a floppy disk in drive A:. This is a leftover from the days of small files which could be stored on

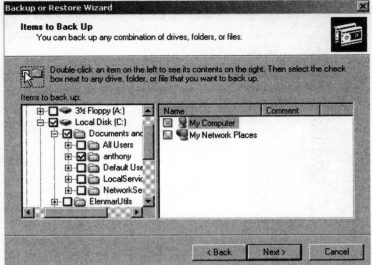

Figure 2.04

small disks such as floppies. It is possible to back up to a floppy or a set of floppies, but if you are planning on backing up any quantity of data this is slow and tedious, besides which floppy disks are also too easily damaged and corruptible to be really useful. Also, many newer PCs don't have a floppy drive installed at all!

Neither version of XP has the ability to burn directly to a CD or DVD recordable drive, so you are effectively left with the choice to back up to your own hard drive, a network drive, or some form of removable mass storage such as a USB flash drive or an external hard drive.

Figure 2.05 shows browsing for a suitable location in Network Places. An alternative, might be to navigate through My Computer to a removable disk or USB pen drive.

Once the destination drive has been selected the final stage of making the backup is shown in Figure 2.06.

Note there is an Advanced button which will allow you to select the backup type such as full, incremental, etc. Backup types are covered in more general terms as part of Chapter 6, *Backup*

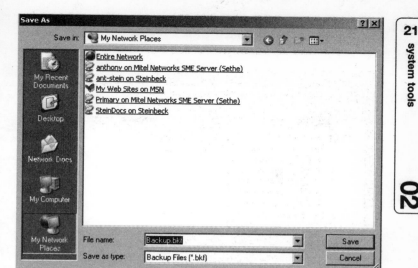

Figure 2.05

Figure 2.06

strategies. For the time being, click **Next** to proceed with the backup. In the next few screens you will be given some options to verify data or to append or overwrite previous backup jobs, and finally, a choice to back up now or later. If you choose the latter, you will be presented with a dialog box which enables you to schedule the backup for a future time and date and to be repeated regularly. (See also the Task Scheduler, below.) You will also be prompted for a password for the backup job. You may leave this blank if you wish.

Once your backup job is running you will see a progress report on screen as in Figure 2.07.

Backup Progress		?✕
		Cancel
Drive:	C:	
Label:	Backup.bkf created 19/12/2005 at 12:00	
Status:	Backing up files from your computer...	
Progress:	▮▮▮▮▮▮	
Time:	Elapsed: 12 sec.	Estimated remaining: 38 sec.
Processing:	C:\...ft Office 2003 Setup{0001}_Task{0001}.txt	
Files:	Processed: 340	Estimated: 2,661
Bytes:	15,811,357	64,448,033

Figure 2.07

Restoring your data

If your data is lost or corrupted you will need to restore it from your backup copy. This is really just the backup process in reverse.

To restore your data you need to start the Backup utility. Either click its icon in System Tools or navigate to the backup file on your storage medium. It will be identified by an icon such as this. Notice that the backup has been given a name indicating the owner of the files and the

anthony-data-
21-12-05.bkf

date. You will have chosen a similar meaningful name or used the default name of *Backup.bkf*. Either way, click on the backup file in order to start the Backup or Restore Wizard.

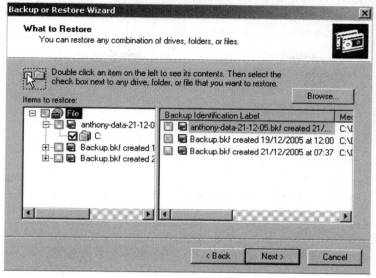

Figure 2.08

The opening screen will be the same as that in Figure 2.04. To run a restore operation click **Next**. The next screen will list the backup jobs that you have previously created. Figure 2.08 shows the *anthony-data-21-12-05.bkf* backup job ready for restoring. Click **Next** to proceed. At this point you can accept the default values – to restore everything to its original location without overwriting existing files of the same name, or you can choose **Advanced** to restore to a different location.

The Windows backup system has several advantages: it is available on all Windows systems and is very flexible in terms of what, where (and even when) you run backup and restore jobs. Probably the best way to get to grips with Backup is to experiment with some trivial files on a floppy disk or a removable pen drive.

Other approaches to backing up your data are considered in Chapter 6, *Backup strategies*.

2.3 Vista Backup

To access the Vista backup utility, navigate to System Tools (from the Start Button, as in XP) and click on the Backup entry in the menu. Vista will display a Welcome screen as in Figure 2.09.

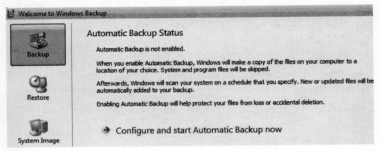

Figure 2.09

The three main functions of the Vista backup system are displayed: *Backup*, *Restore* and *System Image*. We will look at each of these in turn:

Backup

This is the same in principle as the XP backup utility, but you can easily automate the process. To set up an automatic backup:

1 Click the **Configure and start Automatic Backup now** option. This will give you a choice of the types of file – documents, photos, etc. – that you want to back up. Make your choice and click on **Next**.

2 You will be given a choice of destination for your backup files. Choose from the drives on your PC – including burning to CD/DVD – or click **Browse** to select a network drive. Make your choice and click on **Next**.

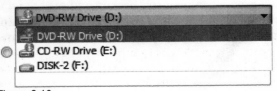

Figure 2.10

3 You will be asked when and how often to run a regular backup job. Make your choices and click on **Finish**.

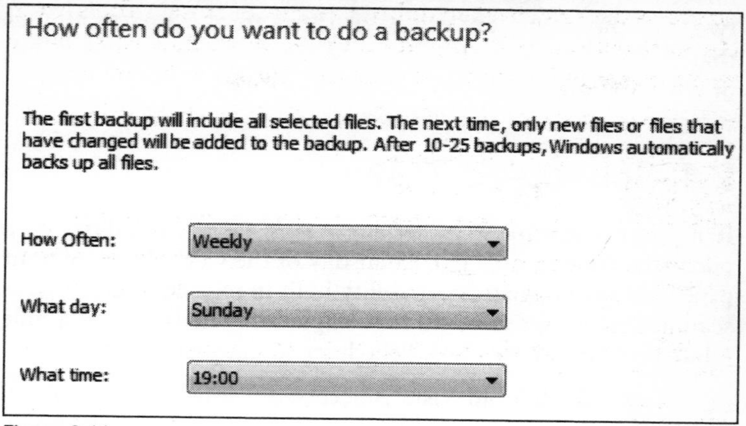

How often do you want to do a backup?

The first backup will include all selected files. The next time, only new files or files that have changed will be added to the backup. After 10-25 backups, Windows automatically backs up all files.

How Often: Weekly ▾

What day: Sunday ▾

What time: 19:00 ▾

Figure 2.11

4 You will be given the opportunity to run a full backup job now, or to defer it until the next scheduled run. Make your choice: **OK** or **Cancel**.

Now that you have set up the backup system for the first time, clicking on the Backup menu entry will allow you to manage future backup and restore operations.

Restore

The Restore function is similar to that of the other Windows versions. Click on the Restore button and navigate to the backup files that you want to restore, select the backup job you want (probably the last one) then follow the instructions on the screen. There is also an Advanced option which will allow you to restore files from another computer.

System image

The choices for this are similar to that of a conventional backup. Choose a destination drive for your system image and follow the instructions on the screen. Because you are making a complete image of your C: drive – Windows, applications programs, the lot – this has to be done on a separate drive, whether a removable disk or across a network. In the event of (say) a hard disk failure, you should be able to fit a new hard drive, restore your saved image and have you whole system back in place in an hour or two. For those who are using XP, there are third-party utilities that you can use to make, save and restore system images, but, of course, you have to pay for them!

2.4 Scheduled Tasks

It is often convenient to set up a task to run regularly at a particular time or on a particular day of the week. Some of your programs may have this capability built in to them – many virus scanners can be set up to check for updates each day, for example – but you can use the Task Scheduler to automate *any* task.

(The Task Scheduler in Vista is accessed through **Control Panel > Administrative Tools** rather than in the System Tools menu. As is often the case, Vista provides much the same functionality as XP, though the user interface looks rather different.)

Like many Windows features, Scheduled Tasks uses a Wizard to guide you through the processes of setting up and managing scheduled tasks. To get started, navigate to the System Tools menu and click on the Scheduled Tasks entry. This will open a window which shows your existing scheduled tasks. Unless you have already set up one or more tasks this will be empty (as in Figure 2.12) and the only option will be to set up a new task.

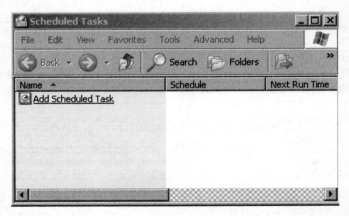

Figure 2.12

1 Click on **Add Scheduled Task** to start the Wizard.

2 Click **Next**. You will be presented with a list of programs which you can schedule to run automatically. There is a **Browse** button which allows you to search for more. Select the application that you want to run and you will be presented with the choices shown in Figure 2.13.

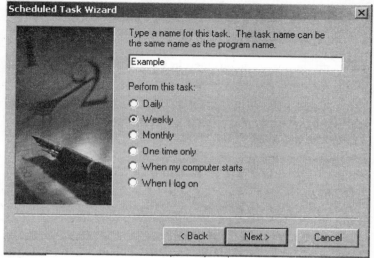

Figure 2.13

Subsequent screens allow you to select the time of day and frequency of the Scheduled Task and to set a password to enable it to run.

Once you have set up a Scheduled Task it should run as and when you have specified. In order to review your Scheduled Tasks, simply start the Wizard and you will see something along the lines of Figure 2.14.

Name	Las...	Schedule	Next Run Time	Last Run Time ▲
🔲 Add Schedu...				
🔲 backup	0x0	At 05:00 every d...	05:00:00 27/12/2005	05:00:00 25/12/2005

Figure 2.14

At this screen you can check that the task ran as expected, modify its settings, delete it if it is no longer needed, or set up a new job.

2.5 Security Center

The Security Center is a feature which was introduced into the XP family with Service Pack 2. It is very unlikely that you will not have Service Pack 2 installed on your XP machine – to check, right-click on My Computer and look at its Properties. The General tab shows (amongst other things) the Service Pack level. If you don't have Service Pack 2 installed, Chapter 13, *Installing/ reinstalling Windows* will show you how to do this.

To access the Security Center in XP, navigate to the System Tools menu and click on its menu entry. In Vista, navigate to the Security Center through the Control Panel.

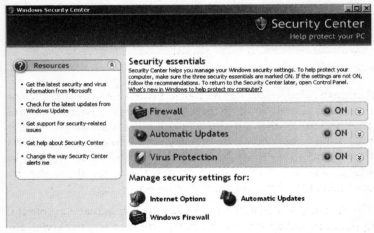

Figure 2.15

Figure 2.15 shows the options for the Security Center. The Panel to the left lists some resources – the first three connect you to the Microsoft website (if you are connected to the Internet), the fourth *Get help* starts the XP online Help facility, the fifth, *Change the way Security Center alerts me*, is shown in Figure 2.16. The screenshot shows the default settings for XP *Security Center* – which is set to issue alerts if there are any settings which may compromise your security. This is probably a sensible setting for many users, but some people may need to change them.

The top three entries in the right-hand panel in Figure 2.15 (Security Center) show the status of the Windows Firewall, the

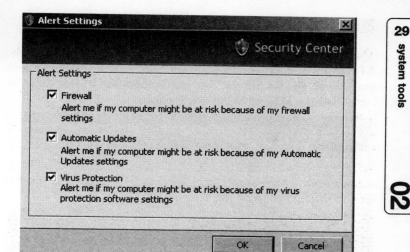

Figure 2.16

Automatic Updates service and Virus Protection. The icons below this panel allow you to change these settings. Chapters 15 and 16 examine security and anti-virus issues in some detail. For the time being, simply note that you may choose to turn the Windows firewall off (the Firewall icon at the bottom of the figure) in which case you may want to disable the alerts about this by unchecking the Firewall Alert box shown in Figure 2.16.

The Automatic Updates icon allows you to manage automatic updates, including turning the service off (not recommended for most users) and the Internet Options allows you to control your Internet Explorer browser settings.

The Security Center gives a common access point for security related settings. However, all of these settings can be accessed elsewhere in the system – such as in the Control Panel, for example, which we will look at in Chapter 3, *Control Panel*.

Note: the Vista Security Center uses the term 'Malware Protection' to indicate anti-virus software and Windows Defender anti-spyware protection.

2.6 System Information

System Information is one of the less commonly used of the System Tools. It provides a lot of very detailed information about the system and its history. The implementation of this utility is all but identical in all Windows versions.

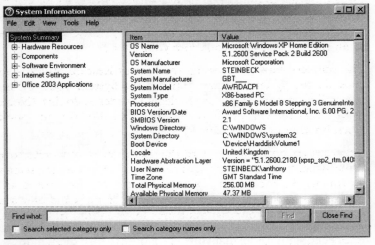

Figure 2.17

Figure 2.17 shows the opening screen of the System Information utility. It has a fairly typical 'Explorer' style interface in which the pane to the right of the display is used to list details from the items in the list on the left. Click on one of the + marks in the list on the left to open it up to show further detail. By default, System Information shows the current information. Selecting View from the menu at the top enables you to list the system's history – which can occasionally be useful for troubleshooting. There is also a Tools menu which gives access to advanced diagnostic tools and the System Restore utility.

Most of the content of System Information – such as System Restore – can be accessed from elsewhere in Windows. By all means use this utility to explore your system, but be aware that most of the information is too detailed to be of much use to most home users and is certainly beyond the scope of an introductory book such as this.

2.7 System Restore

System Restore is concerned only with system files. Its operation is the same in all Windows versions. Word processing files, pictures, emails and other data files are not affected by this utility. This means that you need to back these items up for yourself using the Backup utility that comes with Windows or by one of the alternatives outlined in Chapter 6, *Backup strategies*. The good side of this is that if you do need to 'roll back' your system to an earlier date, you won't lose your data.

The simplest way of accessing the System Restore utility is to click on the System Restore entry in the System Tools menu. You will need Administrator privileges in order to do this. (Note: in XP Home the System Restore utility is also offered as an option when booting into Safe Mode.)

Regardless of how you get there, the operation of System Restore is the same. It monitors changes to the system behind the scenes as you work, and creates restore points. In effect, these are backups of important system and Registry settings and they are created every 24 hours without user intervention. In addition, Windows sets a restore point before any critical changes are made to the system, such as installing new drivers or a Service Pack. You can also set your *own* restore points before undertaking a critical task.

When you click on the System Restore entry in the System Tools menu, System Restore starts in Wizard mode. It offers the options:

◆ Restore my computer to an earlier time

◆ Create a restore point

◆ Undo my last restoration.

The third of these options is only present if you have already carried out a restoration operation and want to 'roll back the roll-back', so to speak.

To restore an earlier system state:

1 Start **System Restore** and select the *Restore my computer to an earlier time* option. You will see a screen like the one in Figure 2.18.

1. On this calendar, click a bold date.   **2. On this list, click a restore point.**

<	December 2005					>
Mon	Tue	Wed	Thu	Fri	Sat	Sun
28	29	30	1	2	3	4
5	6	7	8	9	10	11
12	13	14	15	16	17	18
19	20	21	22	23	24	25
26	27	28	29	30	31	1
2	3	4	5	6	7	8

<	27 December 2005	>
	There are no restore points created yet for this day. To restore immediately, pick another day and restore point, and then try again.	

Figure 2.18

2 Select a date. You will then be presented with a screen like the one in Figure 2.19.

1. On this calendar, click a bold date.   **2. On this list, click a restore point.**

<	December 2005					>
Mon	Tue	Wed	Thu	Fri	Sat	Sun
28	29	30	1	2	3	4
5	6	7	8	9	10	11
12	13	14	15	16	17	18
19	20	21	22	23	24	25
26	27	28	29	30	31	1
2	3	4	5	6	7	8

<	18 December 2005	>
	19:08:21 System Checkpoint	

Figure 2.19

3 The system tells you the time and date that the restore point was set and the reason – in this case a routine system 'snapshot'. Click the **Next** button.

4 You will see a screen that issues a final warning. Select **Next** to start the process. Your system will appear to do nothing for a few seconds and will then close down. It will display a *System Restore* progress indicator on screen, then finally close down and restart in the normal way.

5 You will be presented with the usual login procedures (or none, if your system is set up that way). Then you will be shown a notice which confirms 'Restoration Complete'. Click **OK** to accept this.

If all has gone well, your system will be working properly. If not, you may be able to restore to an earlier restore point or even to reverse the restore which you have just completed. Start the System Restore utility and follow the instructions on the screen.

Setting your own restore points

Although Windows makes a pretty good job of saving your settings, it may be wise to set your own restore point before doing a job such as a major software installation.

1 Start the System Restore utility, select the *Create a Restore Point* option, then click **Next**.

2 You will be given the opportunity to add a description of your restore point and this will be added to the time and date information attached to it.

3 Click **Create**. Windows will create the restore point and confirm this. Click **Home** to go back to the Wizard, or **Close** to finish.

If you start the System Restore Wizard again you will see the new restore point which you have created. Figure 2.20 shows a custom restore point.

1. On this calendar, click a bold date.   2. On this list, click a restore point.

<	December 2005					>		<	27 December 2005	>
Mon	Tue	Wed	Thu	Fri	Sat	Sun		11:39:32 Demonstration for Teach Yourself Book
28	29	30	1	2	3	4	
5	6	7	8	9	10	11	
12	13	14	15	16	17	18	
19	20	21	22	23	24	25	
26	27	28	29	30	31	1	
2	3	4	5	6	7	8	

Figure 2.20

2.8 Files and Settings Transfer Wizard

The *Files and Settings Transfer Wizard* is one of the less frequently used *System Tools*. It was introduced into Windows with XP and is intended to make it easier for users to migrate their data and settings from an earlier machine, including machines running earlier Windows versions such as Windows 95, Windows 98, Millennium or NT 4.

You may want to use this facility to transfer files and settings from an older machine to some form of intermediate storage such as an external disk drive, or by connecting the old and new machines directly using a laplink-style cable (*not* recommended

– it takes forever) or across a network connection. If you don't have a network as such, now may be the time to have a go by setting up a simple two-node network on a crossover cable. See Chapter 17, *Home networking*.

You may also want to use the Files and Settings Transfer Wizard in the course of installing or reinstalling your operating system. See Chapter 13, *Installing/reinstalling Windows*.

The Vista version of this utility is the *Migration Wizard*. As with other utilities that we have looked at, the Vista version provides much the same functionality as XP but through a newer user interface.

Summary

In this chapter we have looked at the most important of the System Tools. Some of them, like the Files and Settings Transfer Wizard or Migration Wizard, you will use seldom if at all. Others, like Security Center or Backup should become familiar through frequent use. There are third-party utilities of course – especially for backup and drive imaging – but the Windows System Tools have the advantage of being available on any and every functioning Windows PC.

As with many (perhaps most) aspects of your PC, the best way of getting to grips with the System Tools is to use them.

03

control panel

In this chapter you will learn:

- how to access the Control Panel
- about the basic functions of the Control Panel tools

3.1 Opening the Control Panel

The Control Panel is a toolbox for your system. Many of the tools can be accessed from elsewhere, such as through the System Tools menu or the Properties of (My) Computer. The Control Panel puts these and other tools together for convenience.

The easiest way to access the Control Panel is through the Start menu option. You should see something like Figure 3.01. This shows the XP Control Panel in Classic View – the Vista Control Panel is similar in appearance. Most people find Classic View easier to work with. If you prefer to work with the (default) Category View by all means do so. Otherwise, click on the Switch to Classic View option. Most of the elements in the example are Windows components installed by the system. One or two others may have been added by applications when they were installed.

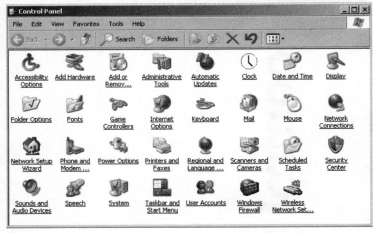

Figure 3.01

For example, in Figure 3.01 there are entries for both Clock and Date and Time. The Clock entry is for a third-party calendar and clock utility which runs in the system tray; the Date and Time entry is the Windows component which allows you to change the system date and time. Similarly, you may see entries for other applications like Nero (CD burning software) or Java (the Java runtime environment). Your Control Panel will look broadly similar, but not necessarily identical, to this.

The items in the Control Panel are 'applets' – that is to say, small applications – and as with all Windows applications, they are launched by clicking on the icons. After that, just follow the instructions on the screen.

The applets are in alphabetical order, so the first is **Accessibility Options**. Clicking on this displays the options shown in Figure 3.02. As with most Control Panel applets, this has a series of tabs, each of which takes you to a page of options. For example, the **Display** tab allows you to change the screen output in various ways – colours, font sizes, contrast, etc. – to improve accessibility for people with visual impairments.

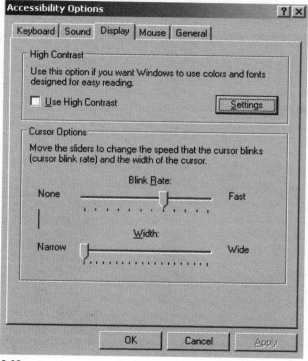

Figure 3.02

This feature is known as the Ease of Access Center in Vista – the visual presentation is somewhat different, but the functionality is pretty much the same.

Whether you are using XP or Vista there are far too many options to discuss them all here. The best way of getting to know your way around is to try a few things and see what happens. If you don't like the results, change them back again – you are in control.

3.2 Customizing your PC

Display

Display settings affect the appearance of your Desktop and can affect performance and usability. Clicking on the Display icon opens the Display utility as shown in Figure 3.03. There are five tabs: Themes, Desktop, Screen Saver, Appearance and Settings.

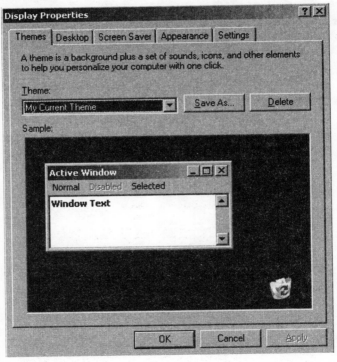

Figure 3.03

The **Themes** tab is concerned with the look and feel of your system and can be altered to suit your own tastes. You can save your current theme by clicking **Save As** and giving it a name. This means that you are then free to experiment with other themes, safe in the knowledge that you can restore your original if you want to. Various themes are provided by default and there is also a More Themes Online option which will take you to a Microsoft site which will offer you additional paid-for themes. Whatever theme you choose, the system will show a preview which you can accept by clicking **Apply**.

The **Desktop** tab is concerned with the appearance of the Desktop. You can choose from a range of backgrounds – including 'none' – and preview them before clicking **Apply**. You can also select a different background colour. The **Customize Desktop** button allows you to change the Windows default settings (see Figure 3.04). Many users like to see icons for commonly used items and to disable the Desktop Cleanup Wizard. Check or uncheck the boxes to suit your preferences.

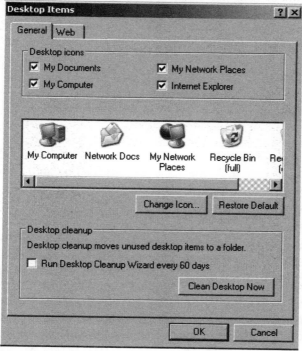

Figure 3.04

The **Screen Saver** tab presents you with a drop-down list of available screen savers. It allows you to set the inactivity interval before the screen saver activates and an (optional) password before the PC can be used again. There is a **Preview** button to preview your chosen screen saver and a **Settings** button for screen savers which are configurable. The **Power** button takes you to Power Options. Most of these are set to reasonable defaults when the operating system is installed and rarely need to be changed.

The **Appearance** tab allows you to change the appearance of Windows. There are three drop-down lists: **Windows and Buttons, Color Scheme** and **Font size**. There is also a preview panel so that you can see the expected results of your choices. For most users the Windows default colour scheme is fine. The ability to increase the font size can be useful for some users.

The **Settings** tab allows you to change the screen resolution and number of colours used in the display. There is no right choice here – choose the settings supported by your system which suit you. The **Advanced** button gives you access to features which are probably best left alone!

Note: the same functionality is available in Vista, but access to it is through the **Personalization** applet in the Control Panel.

Date and Time

You need to be the Administrator to use this utility, though XP Home users need not worry about this as they have Administrator rights by default. As the name suggests the Date and Time applet allows you to change the date and time settings on your system. The interface presents you with three tabs: Date and Time, Time Zone and Internet Time.

The most commonly used tab is **Date and Time** where the clock and calendar can be set. **Time Zone** may need to be reset from the default *US & Canada* if this was not done while (re-)installing the operating system. The **Internet Time** tab allows you to update the system time by clicking the **Update Now** button. This synchronizes your system clock with an atomic clock which is used as an Internet Time Server. Ticking the box *Automatically synchronizes with an Internet Time server* will run the

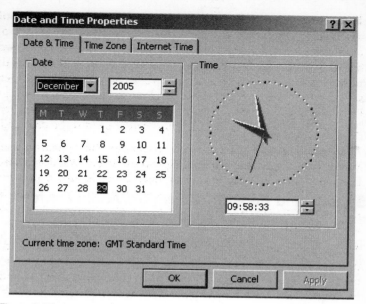

Figure 3.05

synchronization process each week. You need to be connected to the Internet at your chosen time for this to happen.

Regional and Language Settings

Regional and Language settings are normally configured when Windows is installed. Selecting a language from the drop-down list selects appropriate values for currency, numbers, etc. Thus, if you select English (United Kingdom), the currency symbol will be set to £ and the comma used as a separator in numbers (as in 1,000,000,000). These values can be customized if you wish. There is also a drop-down box which allows you to select your *current location* so that information services such as news and weather can be localized for you.

Taskbar and Start Menu

This applet gives you access to the properties of the Taskbar and Start menu. This is an alternative to right-clicking on the Taskbar and selecting **Properties**. The Start menu tab allows you to choose between the default and the Classic Start Menu. Whichever option you choose, there are further options available through the **Customize** button. There are many choices available and the best way to decide is to experiment, find what you like, and stick with that.

The Taskbar tab allows you to reset the Taskbar. When Windows is newly installed it has default options which many people find inconvenient and you may wish (say) to unlock the Taskbar, enable the Quick Launch toolbar, and show the clock in the System Tray. Again, experiment, find what you like, and do that.

Sounds and Audio Devices (XP)/Audio Devices and Sound Themes (Vista)

This gives you access to settings for your sound card and attached devices such as microphones or speakers. Most of the settings are intuitively obvious: a slider control for volume settings on the speakers, volume controls for input devices such as microphones or drives. The second tab **Sounds** allows you to change the default sounds which Windows makes in normal operation – such as the Startup and Close-down music. This can be disabled by selecting **No Sounds** from the drop-down list and clicking the **OK** button.

Keyboard

This option does very little. It allows you to set the length of time you need to hold down a key before it starts to repeat, the speed at which repeated characters are output to the screen and the blink rate of the cursor. Most keyboard problems which you will encounter are problems with Country or Location settings. For instance if pressing the £ key prints out a # symbol then you have a US rather than a UK keyboard. To fix this, go to the Regional and Language Settings applet (see above).

Mouse

The Mouse applet gives you the facilities to fine-tune the operation of your mouse. You can, for example, switch the left and right mouse buttons (useful, perhaps, if you are left-handed), you can change the pointers which the system displays, the speed at which the pointer moves and turn 'trails' on or off. There is an option (under the **Wheel** tab) to control scrolling behaviour which is particularly useful for ease of reading online documents such as newspapers.

The **Pointers** tab gives you access to a drop-down list of Schemes – predetermined themed groups of pointers – which includes novelty items such as Conductor and Dinosaur.

Game Controllers

This applet lists any games controllers such as joysticks or gamepads which you have installed. It also provides the facility to install a new game controller device. If you do this, make sure that you read any manual or installation instructions that come with the device before attempting to install it.

3.3 The options applets

Folder Options

This applet has three tabs: General, View and File Types.

The options available from the **General** tab are fairly self explanatory. Try them and see what suits you and your way of working. There is a **Restore Defaults** button if you don't like the results of your changes.

The **View** tab allows you to change such things as which files are visible in day-to-day use. By default, Windows doesn't display hidden or system files (not a bad idea for many users) and doesn't show file extensions. Thus the filename of the Word file *myfile.doc* is shown without its extension as *myfile*.

If you wish to change these settings you can do so, safe in the knowledge that there is, once again, a **Restore Defaults** button.

The **File Types** tab allows you to change the relationship between a file extension and the program which opens it. There isn't a **Restore Defaults** button in this section so proceed with care, if at all.

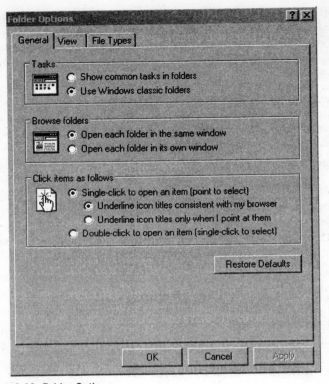

Figure 3.06 Folder Options

How file types work

A filename consists of some text (which means something to the person who created the file) and an extension – nearly always of three characters – which means something to the operating system. For example *CH-03-ControlPanel.doc* indicates to the human reader that the file concerned is the text of Chapter 3 and that the subject of that chapter is the Control Panel. The file extension *.doc* identifies it as a Microsoft Word document. Windows sees this file extension (even though it may be turned off for the user) and knows that it should open *CH-03-ControlPanel* with the application Microsoft Word.

Generally, file associations of this kind work quietly behind the scenes and make life easier. There are, however, times when you may want to change a file association, for example if a 'wrong' one is causing you problems. Suppose that some freak event (and they do happen) has caused your Word files to become associated with another program such as Acrobat. If this happens, clicking on a Word file will launch the Adobe Acrobat Reader which will then fail as it tries to open a file type which it doesn't recognize. Figure 3.07 shows the error message in this scenario.

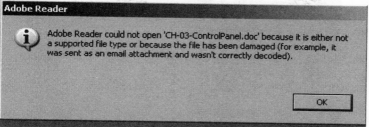

Adobe Reader

ⓘ Adobe Reader could not open 'CH-03-ControlPanel.doc' because it is either not a supported file type or because the file has been damaged (for example, it was sent as an email attachment and wasn't correctly decoded).

OK

Figure 3.07

In this instance, the fact that clicking on a Word document launches Acrobat tells us that the *.doc* extension is associated with the wrong application. To check and change this:

1 Go to **Folder Options**, select the **File Types** tab and scroll down the list until you find the *.doc* extension (Figure 3.08).

Folder Options ?☒

General | View | File Types

Registered file types:

Extensions	File Types
🗎 DESK...	DESKLINK File
🗎 DET	Office Data File
🗎 DIB	Bitmap Image
🗎 DIC	Text Document
🗎 DIF	Microsoft Office Excel Data Interchange Format
DOC	DOC File
🗎 DOC	Microsoft Word HTML Document

New | Delete

Details for 'DOC' extension

Opens with: 🗎 Adobe Reader 7.0   Change...

Figure 3.08

2 Select it and click **Change**. You will see something like this.

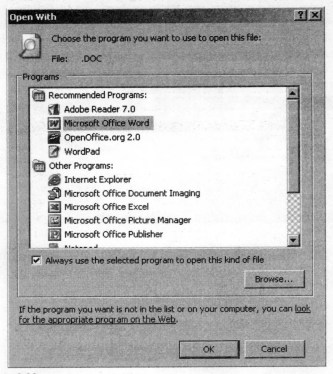

Figure 3.09

3 Scroll down the list of programs, or use the **Browse** option, to find the program you want to use to open files of the *.doc* type. Select it and, if you want to make the new association permanent tick the **Always use ...** box, then click **OK**.

Power Options

Power Options are used to conserve electrical power when the system is turned on but not in use. Laptop/notebook systems in particular need these set correctly to extend the working life of the battery. Figure 3.10 shows the Power Options with an open drop-down list showing the preconfigured options for various system types. All of these can be further configured by the user. Figure 3.11 shows the choices for a laptop/notebook system.

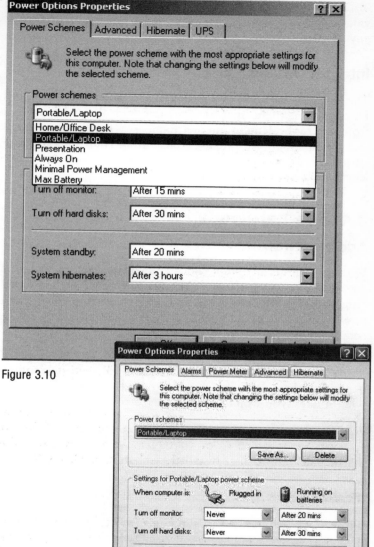

Figure 3.10

Figure 3.11

Windows is usually pretty effective at setting up sensible default values when it is installed so you probably won't need to change any of these settings.

Internet Options

The Internet Options applet gives you access to all of the options for connecting to the Internet. The same controls can be accessed from the Tools menu in Internet Explorer. There are seven tabs and multiple options, ranging from setting your home page to various security settings. These topics are considered at some length in Chapter 15, *The Internet and email*.

3.4 The hardware

Add Hardware

With luck, this is an option which you will never need. Since the days of Windows 95, Windows operating systems have supported Plug and Play (PnP) and this has developed from the hit and miss affair (often called plug and *pray*) of the early days to the robust utility that we enjoy today.

The Add Hardware Wizard scans the system for recently installed hardware that has not 'plugged and played' – an uncommon experience these days. If you want to run the Wizard just to see what it does, you won't do any harm to your system.

Printers and Faxes (XP)/Printers (Vista)

Starting this applet lists installed printers on your system and gives you access to the Add Printer Wizard. The process of installing a printer is described in Chapter 11, *Printers*.

Mail

This is an extension of the Outlook mail and calendar program that is part of the Microsoft Office suite. It provides the facilities to create or modify email accounts. If this option does not appear in your Control Panel this is probably because you don't have the Outlook component of Office installed on your system.

Many XP users use the Outlook Express program for email. Windows Mail is an enhanced version of Outlook Express in Vista. Both of these come free as part of their Windows packages.

Email settings: account names, server addresses, passwords, etc. are outlined in Chapter 13, *Installing/reinstalling Windows* and Chapter 15, *The Internet and email*.

Network Connections

This shows network connections on your PC and will vary quite a bit between different machines. Figure 3.12 shows a machine with two network adapter cards, one of which is disconnected. Right-clicking on the connected network card displays its properties.

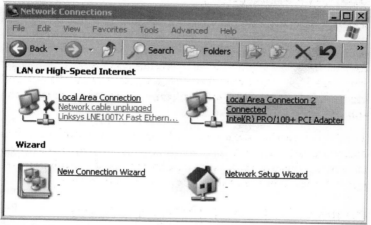

Figure 3.12

In addition to the network cards, there are also two Wizards – the New Connection Wizard and the Network Setup Wizard. The **New Connection Wizard** offers options to connect to the Internet or the local network, or to set up a home or small office network, or set up an advanced connection, although the option to set up a network simply launches the **Network Setup Wizard**.

Networking is similar in Vista, though as you may expect there are some additional options. The starting point to explore these is the Network Center applet in the Vista Control Panel.

Networking – both local and Internet – is the subject of Chapters 17 and 15. For the time being, note that Wizards are not always the best way of setting things up.

Wireless Network Setup

This applet launches the Wireless Network Setup Wizard. This is covered in Chapter 17, *Home networking*.

Phone and Modem

This option is used for setting up a dialup modem connection to an Internet Service Provider. This is the subject of a section of Chapter 15 under the heading of *Setting up a dialup modem*.

Scanners and Cameras

This lists installed digital imaging equipment such as cameras and scanners. It provides access to a Wizard to install new equipment that was not detected at boot time.

3.5 The System applet

Clicking this applet has the same effect as right-clicking on (My) Computer and selecting Properties. We have looked at some of these in Chapter 1. Figure 3.13 shows the output of the applet on a Windows XP Home system with Service Pack 1 installed.

The **General** tab provides basic information about the system and can be a good starting point when working on it. A glance at Figure 3.13 is sufficient to suggest that installing Service Pack 2 may be a good idea for this machine.

The **Computer Name** tab shows us that this machine is called 'Steinbeck' and is a member of the Workgroup Elenmar. These values can of course be changed. On the 'Professional' releases of Windows there is also an option to join a domain. Domain-based networks are beyond the scope of this book.

The **Hardware** tab provides access to the Add Hardware Wizard which is also available through its own Control Panel applet. The **Driver Signing** button that you will find here allows you to control the level of warning that the system gives before installing

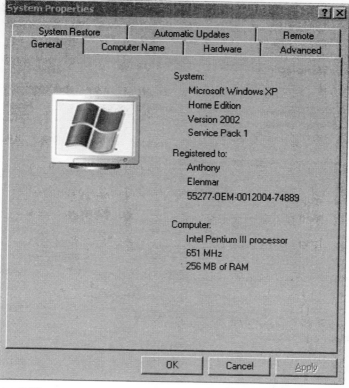

Figure 3.13

an unsigned device driver. This is a scheme whereby Microsoft test and approve – 'sign' – a device driver for, say, a modem, or sound card, or other add-on. A signed driver is guaranteed to work – an unsigned one may give you problems. However, many major manufacturers don't bother with the scheme and it is not uncommon for installation instructions to tell you simply to ignore any warning from Windows about unsigned drivers.

The **Device Manager** button shows a list of hardware devices present on your PC. The top level entry is the name of the PC itself and below it there is a list of devices. When everything is working as it should be, the list is closed up (as in Figure 3.14). If there is a problem with a device it will be marked by a yellow 'blob' and its part of the list will be open as in Figure 3.15.

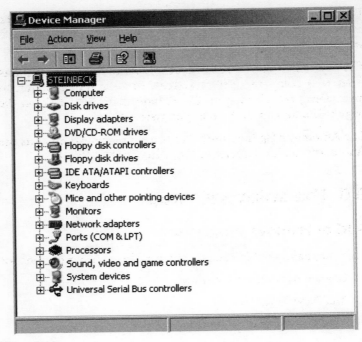

Figure 3.14

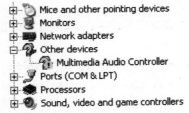

Figure 3.15

Figure 3.15 shows that there is a problem with a Multimedia Audio Controller. The ease and simplicity of this mean that Device Manager is one of the first places to look when investigating a problem with your PC.

The **Hardware Profiles** button is unlikely to be of interest to most home users.

The **Advanced** tab, too, contains little of interest to most home users other than the Performance/Visual Effects setting which we looked at in Chapter 1.

The **Remote** tab allows you to enable Remote Assistance requests from your computer. This is unlikely to be of much interest to most users, but clicking on the Remote Assistance link on the page will take you to the relevant system Help page.

The **Automatic Updates** tab takes you to the same options as the Automatic Updates applet in the main Control Panel.

3.6 The software setup

Add or Remove Programs

This is a major tool in the Windows toolbox. It has options to:

* Change or Remove Programs
* Add New Programs
* Add/Remove Windows Components
* Set Program Access and Defaults.

Given the importance and complexity of this feature it receives an extended treatment in Chapter 12, *Components and programs*.

Automatic Updates (XP)/Windows Updates (Vista)

Like any operating system, Windows is in a continual state of development as new features are added and security vulnerabilities are patched. Microsoft make these available through their website and they can be downloaded free of charge to keep your system up to date.

Figure 3.16 shows a system which is set up to download and install updates at 3 o'clock in the morning every day. This is a reasonable option if you are connected to the Internet 24/7 through an 'always on' broadband connection. Usually, the updates download and install themselves and you don't even notice. Occasionally, you will come to the computer in the

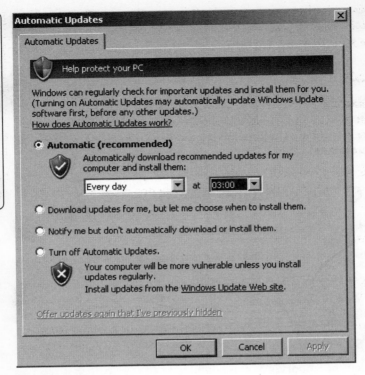

Figure 3.16

morning to find that it has rebooted in order to finish an update. Apart from noting the fact, you need do nothing else.

An alternative is to allow Windows to download the updates but to choose when to install them yourself.

Another possibility is to set the system to notify you of updates but not to download or install them. This option can be useful if you have a slow (typically dialup) Internet connection. For example, you may just dial in a couple of times a day to check email. If this is your pattern of use, fully automated updates are a nuisance. Your best bet, in these circumstances, is to download your mail, do your business, and then choose whether or not to download the updates when you have finished.

The final option in the Automatic Updates is to turn the service off. If you do this you can connect manually to the Windows

Update site by clicking on the **Windows Update Web site** link which appears just below the warning notice advising you not to turn off Automatic Updates.

Fonts

This lists the fonts available on your system. Clicking on a font displays a sample of it using the traditional phrase 'The quick brown fox jumps over the lazy dog' and the numerals 0–9, in various point sizes.

To install a new font, simply drag and drop the font file from the source – a floppy disk, perhaps, or the download area on your system – to the Fonts applet's window.

Speech

This applet is used to set the default voice for text-to-speech programs. By default the system will use Microsoft Sam for synthesized speech. There is a test phrase 'You have selected Microsoft Sam as the computer's default voice' so that you can preview its operation. You can, however, type a phrase of your own in this box, and clicking on the **Preview Voice** button will cause the machine to read out your phrase.

Note: Vista has speech recognition software as part of the operating system and the equivalent of the XP Speech option is the Text-to-Speech option which can be accessed through the Speech Recognition applet.

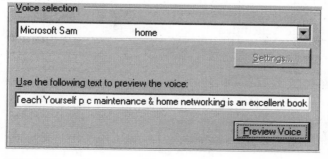

Figure 3.17 (And yes, it can expand the & into the word 'and'!)

Administrative Tools

Most of these are advanced features intended for System Administrators. As a home user you will probably never need to access the Security features in Event Viewer, though you may find it interesting to have a look. More usefully, perhaps, you can partition and format a newly added disk drive by using the Disk Management features (which you can access through the Computer Management shortcut) or defragment your existing disk partitions.

3.7 Security

Security Center

Like the Scheduled Tasks applet, Security Center simply provides access to the Security Center functions which we looked at as part of the System Tools topics in Chapter 2.

Windows Firewall

The Firewall applet gives you access to the same settings and options as in the Firewall option in Security Center.

Scheduled Tasks

This is simply a different starting point for the Task Scheduler which we looked at in Chapter 2 under the *Scheduled Tasks* heading.

Note: the Scheduled Tasks feature is accessed through the Administrative Tools applet in Vista.

System Restore

The *System Restore* tab allows you to set the amount of disk space for storing system information used by the System Restore utility which we looked at in Chapter 2. You are unlikely to want to change any of these settings except to turn off System Restore altogether. This is something which may be necessary as a temporary measure when cleaning up a virus infection. If you do this, all previous restore points will be lost and, after the cleanup, you should turn System Restore on again and make a new restore point immediately.

3.8 User Accounts

Separate User Accounts for people who share the same PC mean that their data and settings – preferences such as Desktop layout and wallpaper – are stored independently. Each user logs on to the machine and sees their own instances of *(My) Documents* and their own Desktop.

Privacy apart, you may wish to have user accounts on the system where system settings, for example, cannot be changed. In order to do this you need Administrator privileges. The example which follows was done in XP Home, but the procedure is broadly similar in other Windows versions.

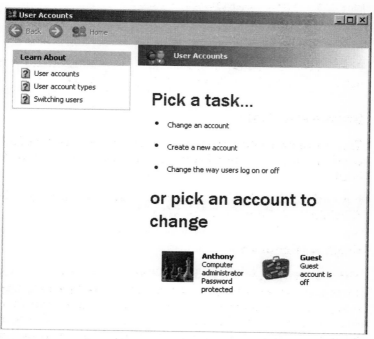

Figure 3.18

To create a new user account:

1 Run the User Accounts applet. This will bring up a screen which shows existing accounts as in Figure 3.18. In this instance we can see that there is a single user account 'Anthony' and a 'Guest Account' which is disabled (a sensible default).

2 To create a new user account click **Create New Account**, and enter a name in the box and click **Next**.

3 Change from the Computer Administrator account type and create a **limited** account. We now have a new user Hilary.

 Anthony
Computer administrator
Password protected

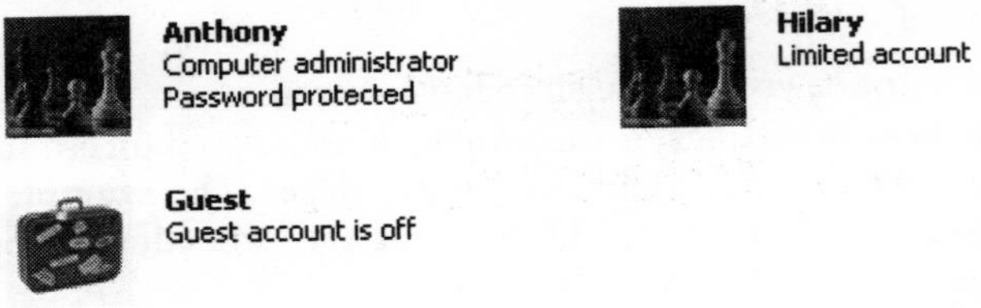

 Hilary
Limited account

 Guest
Guest account is off

Figure 3.19

This account name will appear on the Welcome Screen or Log On Box (whichever your system is set up to use) and on the top of the Start menu. The account will have its own Desktop, Internet Explorer settings, etc. but will not have sufficient rights to alter system settings or carry out tasks such as defragmenting a disk. This can be useful, especially for a family PC where young children have access.

Separate user accounts are the basis of a lot of PC security and are the basis for setting up *Parental Controls* in Vista.

3.9 Parental Controls (Vista)

This is a feature of the Vista version of Windows. They may only be applied to a non-administrator-privileged user account.

To set up Parental Controls for a non-privileged user:

1 Click the Control Panel applet Windows Parental Controls.

 Windows Parental Controls

Figure 3.20

2 You will see a list of users. Click on the name that you wish to control access for. You will be offered these options.

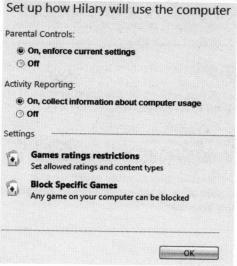

Set up how Hilary will use the computer

Parental Controls:

⦿ **On, enforce current settings**
◯ Off

Activity Reporting:

⦿ **On, collect information about computer usage**
◯ Off

Settings _____

🔧 **Games ratings restrictions**
   Set allowed ratings and content types

🔧 **Block Specific Games**
   Any game on your computer can be blocked

[OK]

Figure 3.21

3 You can fine-tune the options. Click **Games ratings restrictions** to control the types of games permitted. Figure 3.22 shows some of the choices available by category.

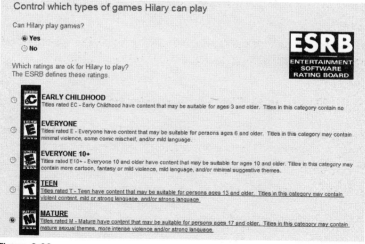

Control which types of games Hilary can play

Can Hilary play games?

⦿ Yes
◯ No

ESRB
ENTERTAINMENT
SOFTWARE
RATING BOARD

Which ratings are ok for Hilary to play?
The ESRB defines these ratings.

◯ **EARLY CHILDHOOD**
Titles rated EC – Early Childhood have content that may be suitable for ages 3 and older. Titles in this category contain no

◯ **EVERYONE**
Titles rated E - Everyone have content that may be suitable for persons ages 6 and older. Titles in this category may contain minimal violence, some comic mischeif, and/or mild language.

◯ **EVERYONE 10+**
Titles rated E10+ - Everyone 10 and older have content that may be suitable for ages 10 and older. Titles in this category may contain more cartoon, fantasy or mild violence, mild language, and/or minimal suggestive themes.

◯ **TEEN**
Titles rated T – Teen have content that may be suitable for persons ages 13 and older. Titles in this category may contain violent content, mild or strong language, and/or strong language.

⦿ **MATURE**
Titles rated M - Mature have content that may be suitable for persons ages 17 and older. Titles in this category may contain mature sexual themes, more intense violence and/or strong language.

Figure 3.22

4 There are further options available to block particular content such as nudity, drug taking or smoking. As with so many aspects of PC work, the best way to find out what you need to know is by experimenting with the options.

Summary

This chapter has looked at the main entries in the *Control Panel* of a typical Windows PC.

With a few exceptions, XP and Vista deliver the same functionality, though they differ in appearance somewhat. Important differences have been noted in the text.

What you should have, after reading this chapter and experimenting a bit, is the confidence to build on the basics and 'Teach Yourself'.

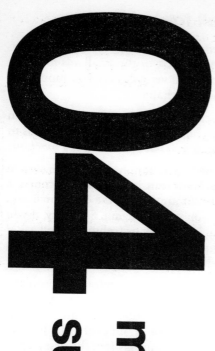

04

making a support call

In this chapter you will learn:

- how to avoid making a support call (if you can)

- how to get the most for your money (if you can't)

4.1 Before you call for help

Sooner or later you will need to make a support call to a Help Desk or look through the phone book or the small ads to find a PC technician. Either of those options will cost you money, so before you do anything, read this chapter.

Whether you are going to tackle the problem yourself or call in an outsider – Help Desk or technician – the first thing to do is to arm yourself with the facts *after you have rebooted the machine*.

There are two reasons for this. First, simply closing the system down and restarting it cures a lot of transient faults. The contents of RAM (main system memory) are lost in the shutdown and reloaded from scratch when you start up again. Secondly, if you haven't rebooted, almost any Help Desk or technician will ask if you have done this, so why pay an expert to tell you this when you can simply do it yourself?

If the reboot doesn't work then you need to define the problem. The Help Desk operator or technician will ask you what the problem is and the clearer you are in your description the less time (and money) you will spend on a support call. Indeed, preparing to make a succinct fault report is often the first step to fixing the problem yourself. Describing – or preparing to describe – something to someone else can be a very effective way of organizing your own thinking.

4.2 Defining the problem

This need not be formal or complicated. What is necessary is to describe what happens or fails to happen. For example, 'I can't connect to the Internet' needs to be fleshed out a bit in order to be useful. Are you using a dialup modem connection or broadband? What, *exactly* do you do which causes the problem to manifest itself? A better description may be something like: 'When I click on the *Internet Explorer* icon on my Desktop, the modem begins to dial then, after half a minute I get an error message "*remote host not responding*"'.

A description along those lines makes it clear that the problem is with a dialup connection and suggests that the problem is probably with your Internet Service Provider – possibly their server is down for some reason.

Your best bet, in that scenario, would be simply to wait for an hour or two and try again later. Or, if you are in a hurry for a result, phone the ISP or use someone else's system to check the ISP's status page on the Web to see if there is a known problem. Figure 4.01 shows part of a status page from a UK-based ISP.

December 20, 2005 13:30 - Dialin Authentication Problems

There have been problems with upstream radius this morning on 0845 6042086 as they are reconfiguring servers and didnt get it quite right :(

If you have problems then we still have our original numbers as backup, detailed on our support page.

Figure 4.01

The support page gives details of known problems and provides a link to further Help. The same information could probably have been obtained through a single brief phone call to the ISP.

4.3 Gathering the information

Whoever you call for help, they will want to know the key facts about your system. It will save you time (and money) to have these facts to hand, so document them before you need them. Write them down and keep a print of the information somewhere safe. There's not much point in having your system details stored on a system that has stopped working! The information that you need might look something like that in Table 4.01.

You could extend this list almost indefinitely or gather more detail if you need or want it. A look at System Information, for example, would give a lot more detail, as shown in Figure 4.02.

Drive	F:
Description	Local Fixed Disk
Compressed	No
File System	FAT32
Size	37.26 GB (40,006,156,288 bytes)
Free Space	9.92 GB (10,654,711,808 bytes)
Volume Name	DISK-2
Volume Serial Number	02521006

Figure 4.02

Item	Details	Source
PC manufacturer	DNUK	Documentation that came with the system Manufacturer's badge on case
CPU	AMD Athlon XP 2000 running at 1.67GHz	Properties of (My) Computer
Installed RAM	1Gb	Properties of (My) Computer
Operating System	XP Professional with Service Pack 2	Properties of (My) Computer
Disk Storage Hard Disk 1 Drive C:	18Gb capacity with 8.35Gb of free space NTFS File System	Properties of (My) Computer
Hard Disk 2 Drive F:	37.2Gb capacity with 9.92Gb free space FAT 32 File System	Properties of (My) Computer
Drives with removable storage	3.5" floppy drive 1 CD writer 1 DVD writer	(My) Computer Or look at the front of the case!

Table 4.01 Information sources

Other useful information are email and ISP login details. You will need to know/find out:

Item	Details
ISP	UKLINUX
Dialup Number	08459042086
User Name	elenmar
Password	********
Incoming Mail Server	pop3.elenmar.com
Outgoing Mail Server	smtp.elenmar.com
Password	********

Table 4.02 Internet login and email information

Passwords

Write them down if you must, but NEVER tell anyone your password over the phone or by email. If absolutely necessary a password can be reset at your supplier's end. If this is necessary, log in as soon as possible afterwards and change it to something that is easy for you to remember but is hard for someone else to guess. It is good practice to use a mixture of upper and lower-case letters and numbers for a password. e.g. 'Fr1day' is an easy to remember variant on 'friday' – easy to remember but hard to guess (at least, it was until somebody put it in a book!)

To find your user name for your Internet connection, just click on the icon that you generally use to connect to the Internet. Figure 4.03 shows details of a dialup connection from an XP Home machine.

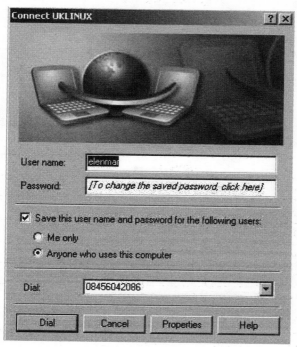

Figure 4.03

Your mail server settings can be obtained from your mail program. As the most popular mail client for Windows systems is Outlook Express, Figure 4.04 shows how to find the settings for that program.

1 Open **Outlook Express/Windows Mail**.

2 Click on the **Tools** entry on the top menu bar.

3 Select **Accounts** from the drop-down menu.

4 Select **Mail** (a tab in Outlook Express – a menu entry in Windows Mail).

5 Highlight your email account.

6 Select **Properties**.

7 Select the **Servers** tab.

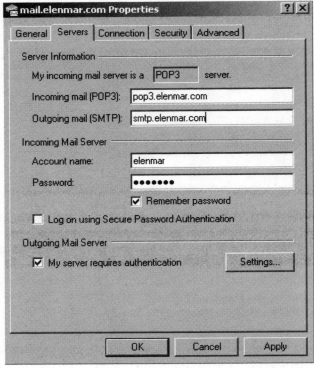

Figure 4.04

If – and only if – the box labelled **My server requires authentication** is ticked (as in the figure), you need to click **Settings** which will take you to a further screen where you can enter separate account details and password for your outgoing mail server. Most home users will not need to do this.

If you are not using Outlook Express/Windows Mail, the procedure for finding the information you require is much the same in the full version of Outlook and other mail clients such as Eudora or Thunderbird.

4.4 Calling the Help Desk

Many of the large High Street retailers offer some sort of warranty or support deal as part of the package. Typically, this requires you to call a Help Desk who will talk you through your problems. These calls are often expensive premium numbers so the more organized you are before you make the call the less it will cost.

Perhaps the most important thing is to have details of the system – make, model number, etc. – to hand along with details of any support contract or warranty you may have. With this in place, dial the number for the Help Desk, describe the problem to the operator and attempt to find a solution together.

Most Help Desk operators are helpful and knowledgeable about their own company's products and will talk you through the process of fixing things. However, they are usually working from a script and can only address a fairly limited range of problems. If, between you, you can't fix a problem fairly quickly, they may suggest running a Restore disk – usually on one or two bootable CDs – which will restore the system to its original factory settings. Such a Restore will destroy all of your data, and installed programs and settings. It may well fix your problem or, if it doesn't, it will have restored the factory defaults so that the Help Desk are now dealing with a machine whose configuration is known to them in detail.

Sometimes, a reinstall – known as 're-imaging' – is the best or even the only way of dealing with a problem. It is, however, a fairly drastic solution, so before doing it have a look at Chapter 13, *Installing/reinstalling Windows*.

4.5 Finding a PC technician

Not everyone has a system which is covered by a warranty or a support contract so, if you can't fix the problem yourself, you will need to find a PC technician to do the job for you. There are three main sources of help for PC problems:

• The High Street names

• Local computer companies

• Sole traders – freelance technicians.

The High Street names

These are the sort of household names that advertise on television and in national newspapers. Most of them offer support and extended warranty services for equipment bought from them. They also accept work from non-customers, but generally require you to take your PC to their premises or charge a hefty premium for a call out to your home. Their hourly rates are generally something like double those of the small local operator. The advantage of dealing with these companies is that they will (probably) still be there next year and that they have a reputation which they care about. They tend to do a good, if somewhat expensive, job. However, they are usually keen to try to sell you upgrades and extras that you may not really need.

A typical offer from one of these chains consists of doing the work – even if it's only a 'PC Health Check' for the quoted price – then advising that the machine 'could benefit from more RAM' and offer to fit it free if you pay for it while they still have the PC in their workshop. It's a fact of course, that just about any PC could benefit from more RAM – it's one of the most cost-effective upgrades that you can do yourself. A stick or two can be fitted in minutes and you can buy them online. The price from one of the High Street retailers is generally something like 30% more than you would pay for it online from the manufacturer: no wonder they can afford to spend two minutes fitting it 'free'.

Local computer companies

A look through *Yellow Pages* or a local directory such as Thomson will generally list several local computer companies.

These vary in size and the services they can offer. Like the High Street names they will probably advertise that their staff have various qualifications (more on qualifications later). The fact that they are in a directory indicates that they are established. They can offer the same advantages as their larger counterparts along with the same shortcomings – higher prices and trying to sell you upgrades you don't really need.

Sole traders

These independent operators will probably give you a better price than the larger companies, mainly because they have lower overheads. Most of them work from home or from small rented premises. When you buy from the High Street or the commercial/business park you are paying your share of the costs of the business rates, not to mention the costs of the glitzy premises.

The independent operators, at their best, can offer you a personal service in your own home for about half the price of the bigger companies. Many of them are skilled and experienced PC technicians; often they are employed in a school or a local authority and do a certain amount of freelance work as a sideline. A handful, though, are cyber cowboys, rip-off artists and clowns. So how do you know which is which?

Word-of-mouth recommendation from satisfied local customers is the best possible indication that someone is competent. If someone known to you can say 'Fred Bloggs did a good job for me' then there's a strong case for hiring Fred to do a job for you.

If no one you know can recommend a technician, then look in the small ads in the local paper or even the postcards in the newsagent's windows or notice boards in a local college. Before making the initial approach, consider the advert. Does it give an address and a landline number, or just a name and a mobile number? Does it say anything about qualifications, the services offered? Does the technician offer a 'no fix, no fee' service?

Having chosen perhaps two or three local techs, phone them and have a chat. Describe your problem in outline and ask if they can help. Ask what their hourly rate is, above all ask if they can give you names and contact details of (say) three local customers for whom they have worked in the past six months. And follow up on this. If you are dealing with a reputable, competent business there won't be a problem in obtaining and checking on customer references.

Qualifications

Qualifications are no substitute for ability and experience, but they *do* matter. The basic qualification for a PC technician is the A+ Certificate from the Computing Technology Industry Association (CompTIA). CompTIA is a Chicago-based organization with members in 102 countries. Its corporate members include global household names like Intel and Microsoft. The A+ Certification is gained by taking two rigorous online examinations designed to test the knowledge of a PC technician with a minimum of six months' work experience. The examinations test the technician's knowledge of hardware, operating systems and the basics of networking. The content of the exams is updated every couple of years to reflect changes in the actual work carried out by CompTIA certified technicians who are working in the field. (Details of all CompTIA qualifications can be seen at their website **www.comptia.org**.)

There are other higher qualifications from companies such as Microsoft and Novell, but these are specific to those companies' own products. There are also, of course, various academic qualifications up to and including Masters degrees in information technology or computing. However, for a practical working tech, earning his or her living in the trade, *CompTIA Certified PC Support Technician* is about the best badge there is.

Summary

This chapter has looked at how to prepare to make a Help Desk call with some tips on how to avoid making that call in the first place.

We have also looked at the business of making a support call when it can't be avoided and how to find a competent local PC technician.

05 the command line prompt

In this chapter you will learn:

- how to access a command line
- the syntax of some common commands
- how to get help with commands
- how batch files and CMD scripts work

5.1 Why use a command prompt?

All versions of Windows support the use of a command line prompt. This is often referred to as a 'DOS prompt' because of its similarity to the original, command-based, DOS operating system which powered the early PCs. Windows replaced DOS and its black and white command line some years ago, and these days we are all accustomed to the point-and-click simplicity of the Graphical User Interface (GUI). The command line, however, can still provide some useful tools for getting things done. A+ certified PC techs all have to be able to use a command line and, while it's not essential for the home user to be able to do so, it can be useful. If you want to, feel free to skip this chapter. If, on the other hand, you want to dig just a little deeper, read on.

5.2 Accessing a command line prompt

The command line prompt is one of the Accessories available from the Start menu on all Windows systems. To reach the prompt:

1 In the **Start** menu, point to **All Programs** then **Accessories**.

2 Right-click on the **Command Prompt** entry in the menu. You will be given the option to *Pin to Start Menu*. You don't have to do this, to use the Command Prompt, but it can be handy to have that – or any other frequently-used item – pinned to the Start menu for quick access.

3 Click on the Command Prompt icon – whether you pinned it to the Start menu, made a shortcut to your Desktop, or navigated to it long hand – to launch the default Command Line Processor CMD.EXE.

```
Command Prompt
Microsoft Windows XP [Version 5.1.2600]
(C) Copyright 1985-2001 Microsoft Corp.

C:\Documents and Settings\Anthony>
```

Figure 5.01

Figure 5.01 shows a command line prompt in XP Home. Note the version number 5.1.2600. The major version number – 5 – indicates that this is Windows XP (Vista is 6). The minor version number – 1 – tells us that this is the second release of Major Version 5 (the numbering starts from 0), and the third number – 2600 – indicates the 'build number' assigned to it by the system developers. All Windows releases use this numbering system to identify themselves.

Directories and folders

These are in fact the same thing. Where Windows refers to 'folders', which contain files (and other folders), the command prompt uses the term 'directory' which is a listing of the files (and subdirectories) which it contains.

By default, the command line prompt shows the current directory (or folder). Thus in Figure 5.01 we can see that the current directory is *Anthony*, a subdirectory of *Documents and Settings* which is, in turn, a subdirectory of the *root*, indicated by the \ (backslash) character. The C: at the beginning tells us that this directory structure is on the first hard disk drive of the system.

5.3 Command syntax

Command syntax is simply the set of rules which govern the way in which a command is used. The general pattern is:

Command [options] [switches] Carriage Return

For example, if we want to see a list of all the files in the current directory, simply issue the command DIR at the prompt and follow it with a carriage return [CR] – (the [Enter] key).

The command DIR [CR] will produce output like this:

```
Volume in drive C has no label.
 Volume Serial Number is 9088-6BAF
 Directory of C:\
04/01/2006  08:40                         0 AUTOEXEC.BAT
05/01/2006  08:00                11,962,447 AVG7QT.DAT
04/01/2006  08:40                         0 CONFIG.SYS
04/01/2006  08:49     <DIR>                  Documents and Settings
```

04/01/2006	08:59	<DIR>		ElenmarUtils
06/01/2006	16:21	<DIR>		Program Files
09/01/2006	08:35	<DIR>		WINDOWS
	4 File(s)	11,962,447 bytes		
	4 Dir(s)	16,011,206,656 bytes free		

The output of the command shows us the drive letter C: and the directory name '\' (i.e. the 'root of C') and a list of files in that directory with their sizes and creation dates. <DIR> indicates that the entry is a directory (folder). The listing ends with a summary of the number of regular files, the number of directories and the amount of free disk space.

If we wanted to list the files of another directory or drive, we tell the DIR command this by means of an option consisting of the command, the option definition and the final carriage return. To see the files on the floppy in the floppy disk drive, for example, the command:

    DIR A: [CR]

will do the job. The 'A:' here is an option indicating the floppy disk drive.

If we want to display the output in wide format, then we use the switch '/W'.

Suggested practical

If you are looking at this material for the first time, you may well be confused by now! The best way to get a feel for the command line is to use one, so:

1 Start a command line processor.

2 Issue the DIR command (don't forget the [CR]).

3 Try some variations on the DIR command like **DIR /W** and **DIR /P**.

4 Look up the Help for the DIR command by typing:

    DIR /?

5 Exit from the command line either by closing the window or by typing **EXIT** [CR] at your command prompt.

5.4 The command set

Some of the DOS commands – like DIR – are common to all systems; others are specific to one or more versions of Windows. In order to explore the command set for your system, start a command prompt and type HELP [CR] – this will list the commands available on your system. You can then obtain detailed help on the command by:

COMMAND NAME /?

Common commands and how to use them

In order to do this exercise safely we will work with a floppy disk. We will also need to create a text file to use in the exercise.

1 To create the text file, right-click on a blank area of your Desktop to get the context menu, and select **New** then **Text Document** as in Figure 5.02. This will create a new text file.

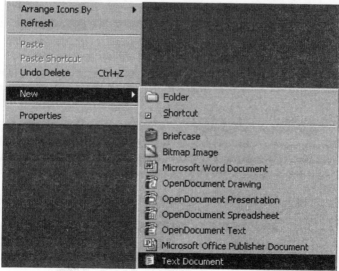

Figure 5.02

2 Click the new Desktop icon to open an editor window. Enter some text like: 'This is a test' or 'Hello World' or anything else you like. When you have finished entering text, open the **File** menu, select **Save** to save the file, then close it.

3 Right-click on the new text file and rename it *newfile*.

4 Put a blank floppy disk in the floppy disk drive.

5 Right-click on the **newfile** icon and select **Send To Floppy**. This will copy the file to the floppy disk in the A: drive.

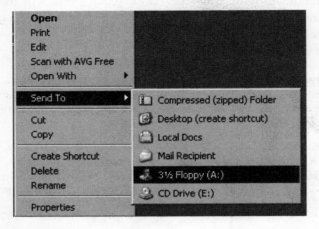

Figure 5.03

6 At the command prompt enter **A:** [CR]. The prompt will now change to A:\> indicating that we are in the 'root' directory of the A: drive.

7 From the A:\> prompt issue the command **DIR** [CR]. This will show a directory listing and you will see *newfile* which you copied earlier. At a command prompt level you can see the full name of the file and its extension, *newfile.txt*.

8 Floppy disks don't often contain subdirectories. But for purposes of the present exercise we will create one called *test*. To do this, we use the MD (Make Directory) command from the A: prompt, like this:

    MD test

9 We can now make this directory current by using the **CD** (Change Directory) command, like this:

    CD test

10 The prompt will now change to A:\test, indicating that we are in the test subdirectory. Issuing the command **DIR** at this prompt will show that the current directory contains no files.

11 To change back to the root directory of the drive use the command **CD **

12 Now copy the file newfile.txt to the test subdirectory by issuing the command

COPY *newfile.txt* [SPACE] *test*

You will see the message '1 file(s) copied'. Changing the directory to *test* and issuing the command DIR will show the new copy of the file in the test subdirectory.

13 To delete the file, issue the command:

DEL newfile.txt

14 Issue the command **DIR** to check that the file has indeed been deleted.

15 Issue the command **CD ** to go back to the root directory of A:

16 Issue the command **RD** (Remove Directory) *test* to remove the (empty) subdirectory *test*

17 Issue the command C: [CR] to take you back to the C: drive.

18 From the C: prompt issue the command

FORMAT A: [CR]

This will reformat the floppy disk, incidentally destroying all data on it.

19 Close your command prompt by typing **EXIT** [CR].

The practical exercise above provides an introduction to some important ideas: the hierarchical 'tree' of directories (folders) on a disk, the commands necessary to navigate between them, and how to create and remove both directories (folders) and files. Finally, you formatted your target floppy disk, thus removing all information on it and preparing it for further use as a clean disk.

The methods and commands used in the exercise can also be used to explore and work with similar structures on your hard disk. If you do this, do so with care. Never use destructive commands like DEL or FORMAT unless you are absolutely sure of what you are doing.

More commands and Help

There are many more commands available at the command line than we have seen here. The Help system will give you some insights into what they are and what they do. If you are interested in command line operations, by all means experiment further, but do so with care. Read the Help entries with care before trying anything – formatting your main hard drive (unless you mean to) is not generally recommended.

5.5 Batch files and CMD scripts

Any command which you type at a prompt may be put in a text file and given the file extension .BAT (a batch file) or the extension .CMD (a CMD script). Batch files use the older command processor COMMAND.COM for backward compatibility with older DOS/Windows versions. CMD scripts use the CMD.EXE command line processor. Thus a file *myfile.bat* will run under the old COMMAND.COM, whereas *myfile.cmd* would run under the newer CMD.EXE. The system chooses the appropriate command line processor on the basis of the file extension.

To create a CMD file of your own, you need to use a text editor which outputs plain (ASCII) text. An ideal editor for this is EDIT.COM. If you want to have a go at writing a CMD script – admittedly a script that doesn't really do much – try this:

1   Open a command prompt in a window.

2   Issue the command **EDIT demo.cmd [CR]**. This creates the file *demo.cmd* and opens it for editing.

3   In the newly opened EDIT window, type in the lines shown in Figure 5.04.

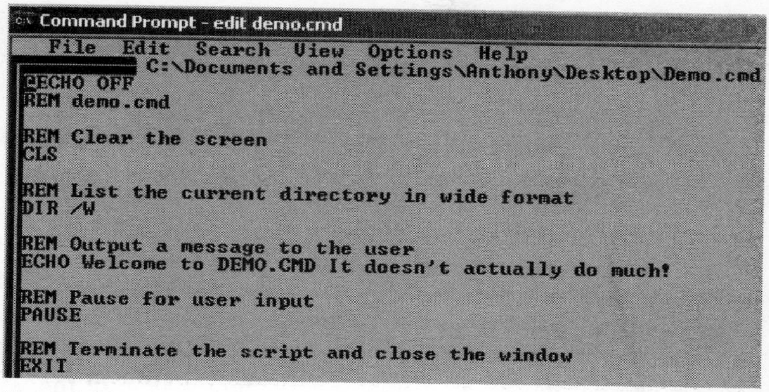

```
Command Prompt - edit demo.cmd
 File    Edit    Search    View    Options    Help
            C:\Documents and Settings\Anthony\Desktop\Demo.cmd
@ECHO OFF
REM demo.cmd

REM Clear the screen
CLS

REM List the current directory in wide format
DIR /W

REM Output a message to the user
ECHO Welcome to DEMO.CMD It doesn't actually do much!

REM Pause for user input
PAUSE

REM Terminate the script and close the window
EXIT
```

Figure 5.04

4 When you have finished adding text as shown in the figure, save the file by opening the **File** menu, and clicking **Save**.

5 Having saved your file, click **File** again and this time click **Exit**. This will return you to a command prompt.

6 To run your CMD file, simply type its name – in this case **DEMO** – at the command prompt. Note that you don't need to type in the CMD file extension for it to work.

7 If your DEMO file doesn't work as it should, make a note of any error messages, reopen the file with the command **EDIT DEMO.CMD** (yes, you *do* need the file extension for this), edit your script, save it, close the editor window and run it again from the command line prompt.

How DEMO.CMD works

The first line of our cmd file is **@ECHO OFF**. This means that the file will not output anything to the screen unless we specifically tell it to do so by using an ECHO command.

The second line begins with a **REM** statement. This is a comment or REMark, i.e. it's there to tell you, or anyone else who is reading the script, what it does: in this case it merely states that the name of the file is DEMO.CMD.

The third line is also a comment which tells us that the next line clears the screen.

The **ECHO Welcome to ...** causes the system to output the message shown.

The **PAUSE** statement causes the system to wait and to output a message 'Press any key to continue' until such time as a key is pressed.

The **EXIT** line causes the script to terminate and closes the window as soon as the user presses any key.

Summary

This chapter has given a brief introductory outline of the command prompt and how CMD scripts work. It is useful background for most users. However, if you are interested in this aspect of your PC you will need to look at some professionally written scripts. If you use the Search utility in Windows – search on *.CMD – you will find a number of scripts on your system. By all means open them with an editor and look at them, maybe even print them off, but don't modify them – they may be important system components.

06 backup strategies

In this chapter you will learn:

- about the types of backup

- how to organize rotating disk sets and archives

- how to back up CMOS/BIOS settings

6.1 Backups

All versions of Windows have some form of *Backup* utility built into them and these were the subject of part of Chapter 2. However, the *Backup* utilities that ship with the various Windows versions do not meet everyone's needs. Neither does making the occasional – or even regular – backup of your files amount to a backup strategy.

Why back up?

Just about everything on your system can be replaced: the applications and programs, even the operating system itself can be reinstalled from their original media (these are the main topics of Chapters 12 and 13). What you cannot replace – *unless you have previously backed it up* – is your own user data: your letters, photos, essays, the chapters of the book you are writing.

The key to a successful backup strategy is to use the media and methods suited to your needs in a systematic way.

Backup media

A backup is just a copy of files and/or settings which have been copied to either a removable medium such as disk or tape, or to another independent system. In the event of a problem with the system, it can be fixed and the lost data restored from the backup copies. It is good practice to store backups away from the PC to which they relate (ideally in another building) so that, in the event of theft, fire, or other accident, the backup copy is safe.

There are many choices of storage media, including:

- Writable CD/DVD disks

- Tape drives

- Removable disk drives – typically hard disk drives which connect through one of the USB or FireWire ports

- Pen drives (not recommended for long-term storage)

- Backing up to another system over a network or even the Internet.

Writable CD/DVD disks

One of the easiest and most popular storage media for use in home systems is the writable – or rewritable – CD or DVD disk. CDs typically hold up to 650Mb of data and single-sided DVDs have a capacity of 4.7Gb. For many users a single disk may be enough to hold all their data.

If all you need to do is back up your own user files, you can use the **Send To** option from the context menu.

1 Right-click on the folder to be backed up (along with all its files and sub-folders) to display its context menu. If a CD burner drive is attached then you have the option of using **Send To** to queue the files to the drive. Windows displays a balloon at the bottom of the screen. Click on this to reach the dialog box to burn the files to CD.

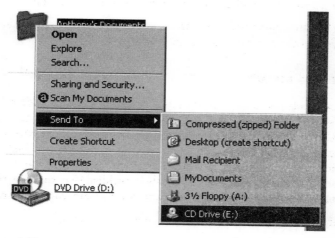

Figure 6.01

2 Alternatively, navigate through My Computer and click on the CD burner drive icon. Whichever route you choose you will be presented with the choices shown in Figure 6.02.

3 To burn the files to the CD in drive E: select the **Write these files to CD** option from the **File** menu. You can also, if you wish, abandon the proposed copy operation by choosing **Delete temporary files**.

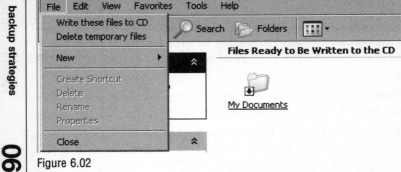

Figure 6.02

The procedure for burning to CD/DVD in Vista is essentially the same: use the **Send To** option from the context menu, or highlight the folders that you want to back up, then select **Burn** from the menu bar at the top of the window.

Figure 6.03

One of the advantages of using this method – providing that your folder and its contents will fit onto a single recordable disk – is that your backup is fully portable. Any machine that can read a CD can read your disk – ideal if you want to read your files on a different machine, even one that uses a different operating system such as Linux or a Macintosh machine with its MACOS X.

If your files take up more than the capacity of a single writable disk you can, of course, choose the **Send to Compressed (zipped) Folder**, then save the compressed file to the burner drive. Although this may not be quite so portable as plain files, most systems can unzip a Windows compressed folder.

Tape drives

There are a variety of tape drives available. They are usually fitted in a spare drive bay on the machine in much the same way as a CD or DVD drive. Tapes are a slow, but high-capacity, storage medium, commonly used for overnight backup jobs of large server machines. Most home users won't need the capacity of a tape drive, but if you are one of the few that do, then have a look at Chapter 8, *Replacing and upgrading hardware*.

Removable disk drives

These tend to be expensive, but can be very useful, especially if you have a lot of data. Usually, they are standard EIDE/ATA hard disk drives in one of the standard capacities – 40, 80, 120Gb or more – housed in an outer case. They have their own external power supply, and the data connection is through either USB or FireWire.

To use a drive of this type, connect its power and data cables and turn on the power. After a few seconds, Windows will detect the new drive and assign it a drive letter. Once this has happened you can drag, drop, copy or delete just as you would with any other drive on your PC. When you are finished, the drive can be disconnected and stored away from the PC.

Pen drives

These are USB devices which will plug and play when you put them into a USB port. Windows detects them, assigns a drive letter, and they can then be used like any other drive on your PC.

Pen drives – sometimes known as 'gizmo sticks' – vary in capacity from 128Mb to 2Gb or more. Because of their small size, they are ideal for moving data between machines or as a short-term backup of files. Because USB is a cross-platform technology, these drives can be read/written to by other systems such as Mac or Linux-based machines. For all their advantages – small size, portability, relatively high storage capacity, these drives are a form of memory – flash memory – and may not be as robust for longer-term storage as other media.

Backing up over a network

If you have more than one PC, you may find it useful to back up data across your network. This can be done manually by copying files using drag and drop, or you may like to write yourself a CMD script to do the job. (Hint: look at the Help for the XCOPY command and experiment with that.)

Another possibility is to back up to an Internet Server. If you have your own web space you may be able to do this by uploading files to your own storage area using the File Transfer Protocol (FTP). Rather easier, perhaps, is to rent off-site storage with a service such as X-Drive, which provides access to secure storage for a monthly fee.

6.2 Backup types

Disk cloning

The ultimate backup is a complete image of your hard drive: data, settings, installed applications, the lot. The best known software tool for doing this is Norton Ghost from Symantec.

Cloning a drive consists of making a byte-by-byte copy of the drive's contents and storing it in a single file which can then be restored in the event of problems. If, for example, you 'cloned' your current system by making an image in a file called *myimage.gho* this would, in effect, be a snapshot of your drive which you could store on a disk drive or a spanned set of CDs. Then, if your current hard disk fails, you can fit a new one and restore your system from your saved image.

This type of restore has the advantage of restoring *everything* – settings, saved passwords, the lot. However you can only restore what you backed up, so if you have deleted unwanted applications or data, they too, will be restored and anything newly installed since the cloning will not be present. Disk cloning can be very useful, but it is no substitute for a systematic backup strategy.

Disk imaging with Vista

Unlike earlier Windows versions, Vista has the ability to make disk images, built into the operating system.

1   Open the **Start** menu, point to **Control Panel**, select **Backup and Restore Center**.

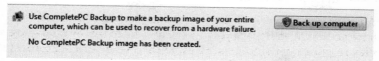

Use CompletePC Backup to make a backup image of your entire computer, which can be used to recover from a hardware failure.

Back up computer

No CompletePC Backup image has been created.

Figure 6.04

2   Click the **Back up computer** button to reach the dialog shown in Figure 6.05.

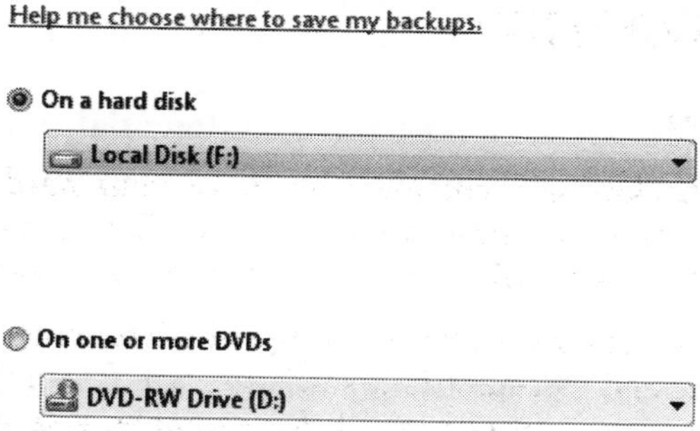

Help me choose where to save my backups.

⦿ On a hard disk

🖴 Local Disk (F:) ▾

○ On one or more DVDs

💿 DVD-RW Drive (D:) ▾

Figure 6.05

3   In this example, the choice is to burn to DVD or to save to a locally attached hard disk. Note that a hard disk used for an image backup must be formatted with the NTFS file system. Click the **Next** button (not shown in the figure) to start the imaging process. The whole of the C: drive will be copied to a single image file on the selected drive. This can be restored in its entirety at a later date. There is no capacity for restoring individual folders or files from it.

4   To restore from an image backup, attach the disk containing your image file, then boot to the **Recovery Environment** (hold down [F8] at boot time). If this isn't possible, boot to your original installation DVD and work from there.

Full backup

As the name suggests this consists of backing up the whole of your system. This is a large undertaking and will require a lot of removable storage space such as a large removable hard disk. It is a job which needs to be done from time to time whether by running a backup program or by cloning the whole drive.

Differential backup

A differential backup copies all files that have been changed since the last full backup. It does not mark the file as being backed up, so it will be backed up again each time you perform a differential backup. If, say, you do a full backup on Monday and a differential backup on Tuesday and Wednesday, then files modified on Tuesday will also be included in the Wednesday backup even though they have been included in Tuesday's. If you have to restore your data on Thursday you will have to use the last full backup and the latest (Wednesday's) differential backup to recover all your data. Contrast this with the incremental backup.

Incremental backup

An incremental backup backs up only those files which have been modified since the last backup of any kind. If you do a full backup on Monday and incremental backups on Tuesday and Wednesday, a file modified on Tuesday will not be included in the incremental backups made on Wednesday. If you have to restore your data on Thursday, you will need to use your full backup, then each of your incremental backups, in date order, to restore all your files.

	Full	Differential	Incremental
Monday	Includes all files	N/A	N/A
Tuesday	N/A	Backs up files modified on Tuesday	Backs up files modified on Tuesday
Wednesday	N/A	Backs up files modified on Tuesday and Wednesday	Backs up only files modified on Wednesday

Incremental backups are more economical of time and storage space and may be useful when backing up a large server, usually using an automated system. For most of us, a combination of full and differential backups are probably the easiest to manage.

Rotating sets

It is usually advisable to have more than one backup for the simple reason that if the backup media are lost or destroyed, then restoring from an earlier backup is better than nothing.

There are a number of systems for rotating sets of backups – full backups and their associated incremental and differential sets – generally in some variant of grandfather, father, son. These arrangements are frequently used in business and commerce, and can be adapted to make a straightforward system which meets the needs of most home users. You will need two, or three, rewritable CDs or DVDs. Label them Disk 1, Disk 2 and Disk 3.

Start by backing up your user files to Disk 1. The easiest way to do this is to use the burning facilities included with Windows (see *Writable CD/DVD Disks*, above). Put a label on the disk cover and record the date of the backup. Put it somewhere safe.

Decide how often you are going to back up – once a week may be enough, or you may want to back up every day – but whatever it is, stick to it. When the second backup is due, write your files to Disk 2, label and date it. When the third backup is due, do the same things with Disk 3.

When your fourth backup is due, erase the contents of Disk 1, burn your backup to the newly erased disk, label it and store it. Ideally, all your backup disks should be stored away from the system, in another room or even in another building. Every month or so, burn a permanent archive disk, label and date it, and store it well away from the system. This may also be a good time to create a system restore point as outlined in Chapter 2.

These arrangements are not 100% foolproof, but they are easy to operate and you can reasonably expect to recover *most* of your data in the event of a failure.

6.3 CMOS/BIOS settings

When you first turn your computer on it doesn't even know that it has an operating system. A chip, somewhere on the motherboard, runs some start-up routines – a basic memory check, detecting hard disk drives, etc. before it loads Windows (or any other operating system for that matter). This chip is known as the BIOS chip – Basic Input Output System.

When the system boots, the BIOS chip runs its built-in programs to set up the system, using information which is held in a small area of a special memory type called CMOS – Complementary Metal Oxide Semiconductor. The information in this CMOS memory is kept alive when the PC is turned off by a small battery, also mounted on the motherboard.

The CMOS battery – which looks like an oversized watch battery around the size of a £1 coin – is recharged while the PC is running and is discharged slowly when the machine is turned off. A flat or dead CMOS battery can cause the system to lose track of the time of day or even to fail to recognize some of its drives.

Replacing a defective CMOS battery is simple. Power down the machine, remove the case or cover, remove the old battery and fit the new one. (See Chapter 7, *Inside the box*.)

When you restart the machine after changing the battery, it may have lost some of its CMOS settings, so it is as well to know what these should be and how to restore them.

Windows does not give you the facilities to backup CMOS settings to a disk, so if you want to do this you will need to use one of the many third-party utilities that are available – searching the web with the terms 'cmos backup utility' will lead you to plenty of them, some of them free.

However, it is really quite simple to access the BIOS/CMOS settings on your machine and write down the key settings with pen and paper.

How to access the CMOS/BIOS settings

Start – or restart – your PC. In the first few seconds you will see some text on screen – white on black, usually – which tells you the name of the BIOS manufacturer and the date that the BIOS was made. There is nearly always a screen message telling you which key to press to enter the Setup Utility – 'Press DEL to enter SETUP' is probably the most common of these, though other keys are sometimes used.

The first time you try this, you may find that the information shoots off the top of the screen before you have time to read it. If this happens, just press [Control], [Alt] and [Delete] all at the same time to restart the PC, and then try again.

When you have found and pressed the right key (or occasionally a key combination such as [Control] + [F2]) you will enter the setup program. Different manufacturers have different user interfaces and often different names for functions, especially for advanced features. However, the basic features are pretty standard.

+ Save and Exit

+ Exit without Saving

+ Standard Features

+ Advanced Features.

The first two options are important when you are working with CMOS/BIOS settings. If you change some settings, you want to save them so that the system remembers them for next time. Equally, if you get yourself in a mess (easily done!) Exit (or Quit) without saving will leave the previous settings unchanged.

The Standard Features option will generally list things like Time, Date, sizes of Disks and Floppy drives. The Advanced Features will list things like Virus Warning (Enabled/Disabled), First Boot Device, Second Boot Device and so on. Make a note of these settings and store them somewhere safe. You may need them in the event of a flat battery.

While you are in the CMOS setup screen, why not take a look around at all those other options that you'll 'never need to use'? Providing you remember to Exit/Quit Without Saving you can do no harm to your system.

Summary

This chapter has looked at backup types – full, differential, incremental and drive images – and strategies such as using rotating disk (or other media) sets. It has also suggested that you should familiarize yourself with, and record, the CMOS/BIOS settings for your system.

There is no definite right or wrong approach to backups. The important thing is to decide what is right for you (and your data) and to carry out your routine regularly. Like checking the tyre pressures on the car or defrosting the fridge, backing up data should be a regular household task.

07 inside the box

In this chapter you will learn:

- how to work safely with hardware

- how to identify the main components

- why some things probably aren't worth upgrading (or replacing)

7.1 Working safely

Modern hardware is generally robust and reliable, though occasionally a component may need to be replaced or upgraded. You may also want to add a component such as a sound card or a LAN card. This chapter and the next introduce you to the main components inside the case and how to work with them. Chapter 8 looks at the tasks of replacing these components in greater detail.

When working with hardware you are unlikely to harm yourself or your equipment providing you follow a few simple guidelines.

The most basic of these is: *always* power down and disconnect from the mains power source before you remove any covers or lids. PCs run on AC mains power – they are no more (or less) dangerous than any other mains powered household gadget.

Once the machine is disconnected from the power, you will need to remove the lid, cover, or side panel in order to access the inside of the machine. Covers and panels are usually secured by two or three screws with a 'star' style head. The best tool for removing them is a Phillips #2 screwdriver. (Occasionally, usually on older systems, you may still encounter torxx screws. In this case you will need to use a torxx driver.)

Having removed the screws, put them somewhere safe: an ashtray or something of the sort is ideal. Next, slide back and remove the lid, cover, or side panel of the machine. If you haven't done this before, the inside of the system probably looks quite formidable. Don't panic – it's not half as complicated as it looks!

Before you touch *any* of the internal components, you should touch a bare metal section of the chassis of the machine. This safely discharges any static in your body – or at least equalizes it with any in the machine – so there is no difference of potential between you and the machine. Having discharged any static in this way, you should always touch bare metal before touching any component. Remember, even though you can't see static it can damage your system.

Wearing a wrist strap which you attach to the chassis of the PC means that you are permanently 'touching' bare metal. If you want a wrist strap, you can buy one for a few pounds from a

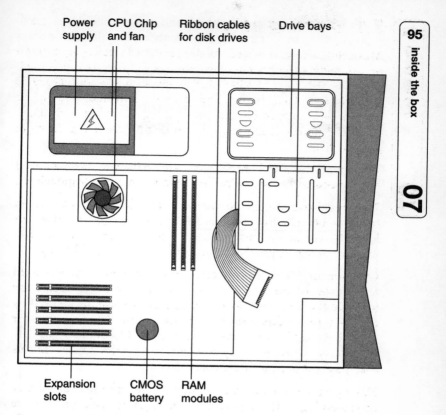

Power supply | CPU Chip and fan | Ribbon cables for disk drives | Drive bays

Expansion slots | CMOS battery | RAM modules

Figure 7.01 Inside your PC

local PC shop. Just remember NOT to wear it if you are in contact with high voltage equipment like a laser printer where it could conduct a high voltage *to* you rather than static *away* from you.

7.2 The main components

Motherboard

The motherboard – sometimes known as the main board, or system board – literally holds the other components together. You can think of it as the communications highway of the system. Every component communicates with the other components on the board through its communications channels, or *buses*. Like most PC hardware it's pretty tough and you are unlikely to need to do anything to it. If it fails, you simply replace the whole unit. Figure 7.02 shows a typical modern motherboard.

At this stage, simply be aware of what the motherboard looks like and the size and positions of its various expansion slots and sockets. Also note any manufacturer's name and serial numbers, though this isn't critical. (There's an easy way to identify your motherboard – see *RAM modules*, below.)

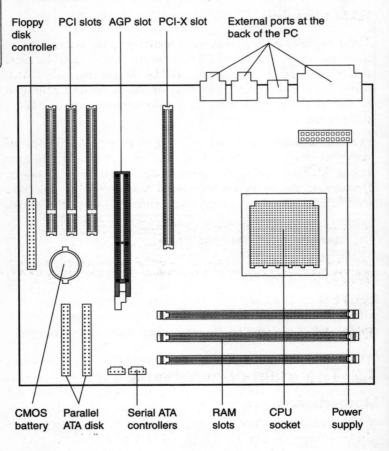

Figure 7.02

CPU

The CPU – Central Processing Unit – is often thought of as being the 'brain' of the system, and sits in a socket on the motherboard. Because of the heat generated when it is running, it is fitted with a heat sink and a cooling fan. If the heat sink becomes clogged with dust or the fan doesn't work, your PC will overheat and stop working within a couple of minutes of being turned on.

RAM modules

These modules make up the main memory of the system. If you have one or more spare RAM slots on the board, then the most cost-effective upgrade you can do will be to add some more RAM. Most PCs bought from High Street or online retailers ship with enough RAM to work, but can usually be improved by adding some more.

Because the major manufacturers of RAM are in the business of selling as much of the stuff as they can, they will make it as easy as possible for you to identify your system and its memory needs. Figure 7.03 shows the results from a free utility downloadable from crucial.com. Note that it also identifies your motherboard.

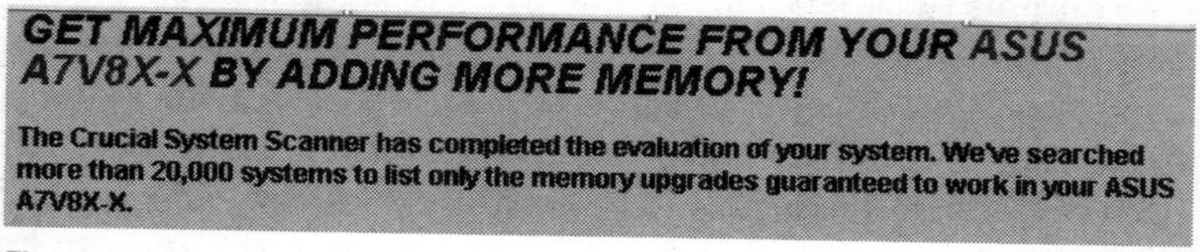

GET MAXIMUM PERFORMANCE FROM YOUR ASUS A7V8X-X BY ADDING MORE MEMORY!

The Crucial System Scanner has completed the evaluation of your system. We've searched more than 20,000 systems to list only the memory upgrades guaranteed to work in your ASUS A7V8X-X.

Figure 7.03

Disk drive controllers

The standard disk drive controller is the EIDE interface – also known as parallel ATA interface. There are usually two of these on most motherboards. Each one has two rows of 20 pins and the surround to the pins usually has a slot so that the data cable which connects it to the drive can only be fitted one way. The cables themselves are usually round in section these days, but older ones may be a traditional ribbon cable. Ribbon cables have a red or pink stripe down one side – this indicates line 1. Where there are two controllers they are designated Primary and

Secondary. Each controller supports two attached devices such as hard drives or CD/DVDs which are designated as either Master or Slave. Sometimes a primary controller is coloured red, blue or green to indicate that it is a higher speed type. This is not, however, an official standard and colours are often inconsistent.

Some newer systems may use Serial ATA (SATA) disk drives. The controllers for these are small rectangular connectors with just seven pins. It is possible to use a mix of SATA and parallel ATA drives, but it can lead to complications and is probably best avoided.

Power Supply Unit

The Power Supply Unit (PSU) converts alternating current (AC) mains power to direct current (DC) which the PC can use. The highest output voltage from the PSU is 12 volts, so nothing 'downstream' of it is likely to do you any harm. The unit itself, however, carries full mains power and should be treated with caution. A PSU is an example of what the trade calls a 'field replaceable module'. In other words, if it fails, replace it as a unit – don't try to open it and fix it – bin it and fit another one!

The outputs of the PSU are to one of three standard connectors. There is a small connector for floppy disk drives (a Berg connector), a Molex connector for other drives such as hard disks, CD-ROMs, etc, and SATA connectors for Serial ATA drives. Of these three power connector types, the Molex is the commonest. It is a general-purpose power connector and can be used to supply power to anything from disk drives to fans. Where a device doesn't have the appropriate connector there is usually an adaptor cable available, for example, you can attach a Serial ATA drive to a Molex connector by using a SATA to Molex adaptor cable. You can also buy splitter and extension cables to increase the number of available power supply connections.

Disk drives

Hard disk drives are usually 40-pin parallel ATA devices or, on newer systems, there may be 7-pin Serial ATA devices. Figure 7.04 shows a Serial ATA disk and connectors.

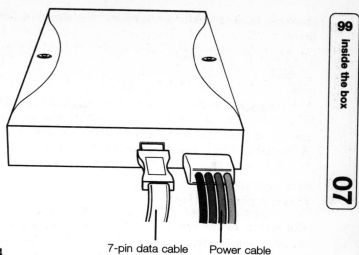

Figure 7.04   7-pin data cable   Power cable

Whichever type your system uses, it will need to be attached to an appropriate power line and a data cable. Power connectors are designed so that they will only fit one way and data cables are usually keyed so that they too, will only fit one way. Some older 40-pin cables may not be keyed, and the rule here is 'pink next to the power'. That is, the red or pink stripe down one side of the ribbon cable which indicates line 1 should be attached to the drive so that it is closest to the power connector.

CD and DVD drives – whether they are read only (ROM) drives or burners – are known collectively as optical drives because they work on laser light instead of the magnetic fields used by hard and floppy disk types. Even the fastest of these are relatively slow compared with magnetic hard drives, so they are frequently attached to the secondary EIDE/ATA controller, especially where this is the slower of the two controllers on the board.

Floppy drives are not fitted on some modern machines and this can occasionally be inconvenient. Chapter 8, *Replacing and upgrading hardware*, shows you how to fit a floppy drive, so now is a good time to inspect your system to see if this is possible.

The first thing to check is that the case has a mount point for the drive. This will probably be a metal cradle about 3½ inches wide near the front of the case and on the outside you will see a blanking plate which is more or less the size of a floppy disk drive.

The next thing to check is the floppy disk controller on the motherboard. There is normally only one of these. At first sight it looks very like one of the hard disk controllers, but is smaller, with only 34 pins. As with hard disk controllers, it will usually be keyed so that it can only be connected one way and where this is not the case, there will be a red or pink stripe on the ribbon cable which indicates line 1.

AGP graphics

Most modern systems use the Accelerated Graphics Port to output information to the screen. There is almost invariably a single slot on the motherboard – brown in colour and not aligned with the other expansion slots – to accommodate a dedicated AGP graphics adaptor card. These vary in size and orientation according to the particular type of AGP card on your system.

Many systems, especially budget systems from High Street or online retailers, have on-board graphics – that is, a dedicated graphics chip connected directly to the motherboard. Most on-board graphics set-ups are suitable for relatively undemanding everyday applications like word processing, email and browsing the Web. Sophisticated high-end games, or Computer Aided Design (CAD) packages may need a high-end graphics card in either an AGP or PCI-X expansion slot.

PCI expansion cards

Peripheral Component Interconnect (PCI) is the standard for most expansion cards on modern systems. The PCI slots on your motherboard are white (or off-white) and there are usually three or four of them. Any PCI card can be fitted in any PCI slot and – given the right drivers – will plug and play 'out of the box'.

A newer standard PCI-X (the 'X' is for 'Express') provides a means of connecting faster PCI-X expansion cards to your system. The PCI-X slot is normally the same colour as the standard PCI slots and is physically longer. There are also two different specifications – versions 1 and 2, with 3.0 under development.

PCI-X is often used as an alternative to the Accelerated Graphics Port (AGP) for graphics output, though it can be used to attach other card types such as high-speed LAN adapters.

CMOS battery

This is a small battery – like an oversized watch battery in appearance – which provides power to the CMOS while the system is turned off. In Chapter 6 we looked at the BIOS/CMOS settings. These settings are kept live when the PC is turned off because the battery provides the necessary power. Rather like the battery on a car, it is recharged when the system is running and discharges when the system is turned off. Repeated charging and discharging will eventually cause the battery to fail. When this happens, a common symptom is that the PC loses track of the correct time. If this happens, then it's time to replace the CMOS battery. These can be bought for a couple of pounds from electronics or electrical goods shops. They are more or less standard components, but an easy way to make sure that you get the right thing is to power down the machine, remove the old battery and take it to the shop and ask for 'another of these'. When you return with your new battery, put it in the holder on the motherboard, replace the case cover on the PC and reboot it. As the machine reboots, press the key to enter the CMOS Setup screen (usually [Delete]) and check that your system has correctly identified the disk drives, etc. You can reset the time and date here as well, but it may be easier to leave time and date settings and correct them through the Control Panel later.

7.3 Why some things aren't worth upgrading

PCs become more powerful and cheaper with every year that passes, and each release of the operating system and other software requires more and better resources. For the first couple of years of your PC's life you can probably keep up with this – a couple of sticks of extra RAM will improve the performance of your PC from day one. You can add to the total RAM count without throwing anything away.

If your hard disk is starting to get full, you can probably fit a second disk to increase you total storage – again, adding capacity without throwing anything away. However, the case for upgrading other components, such as the CPU, is not so clear cut. Suppose, for example, you were to buy a new CPU chip that was (say) 20% faster than your existing chip.

1   Is the chip compatible with other components on your system, especially the motherboard? Check with the motherboard manual and/or the manufacturer's website.

2   Will the 20% faster chip result in a 20% increase in the overall performance of the system? The answer here is almost certainly 'No'.

3   What do you do with the component you are replacing? Sell it? Throw it away?

In general, you need to ask yourself whether in a world of ever-decreasing hardware and system prices, an upgrade is worth the effort and cost of doing it compared with replacing the computer.

Replacement, on the other hand, may well be cost-effective particularly on a relatively new machine where a component has failed. If, for example, your CPU chip has failed, you have no choice but to abandon the old one. The cost calculation here is simply whether it will be better to fit a new chip – possibly even a slightly faster one, a sort of 'incidental upgrade' – or abandon the old system altogether and buy a new one. The decision is more to do with finance than technology as such.

Summary

This chapter has looked at the internal hardware components of a typical PC – what they look like, what they do and how to work safely with them. In the next chapter we will consider the principal components in a bit more detail and will look at the practicalities of replacing them.

08

replacing and upgrading hardware

In this chapter you will learn:

- how to organize your work space
- what tools you need
- how to replace individual components

8.1 Before you start

Hardware components fit together like children's building blocks. Most components fit only in the slot or socket for which they are designed and on modern systems they are usually keyed so that they only fit one way round.

Organize your work space

Time spent on preparation is seldom wasted, so before you start taking things to pieces consider both where and how you are going to work. Clearly, if you are going to do a straightforward job such as adding a stick or two of RAM you will need no more than space to lay the PC on its side, remove the cover and add the RAM. If, on the other hand, you are going to change the motherboard, you will need plenty of space to work and to store the many components that you'll have to remove from the system.

The ideal work space will have a large flat work surface such as a table or bench with adequate lighting. A desk lamp which can be pulled over the work area as needed can be useful, as is a magnifying glass and a small torch for reading small print on components that are buried deep inside the case.

A pen and paper for writing down settings or the position of cables and connectors is pretty much essential for all but the smallest jobs. Some people also use a digital camera to photograph these things.

You will need a Phillips screwdriver – preferably a #2 size – but it is also helpful to have a flat-blade screwdriver, a pair of fine-nosed pliers and one or two small containers such as ashtrays or yoghurt pots for the temporary storage of screws, jumpers or other small parts. Larger parts can often be stored in the upturned lid of the PC. If you are fitting a new component, leave it in its anti-static packaging until you are ready to use it.

Unless you have a dedicated work area like a garage, make sure you allow enough time to do the job. If you are working on the kitchen table and your spouse or kids have to kick you out in order to cook a meal, it will add greatly to the complexity of doing the job. As a rule of thumb, estimate how long it will take you to do the job, then double it, then add an hour!

8.2 How to add RAM modules

Most PC systems are sold with enough RAM to work but will give better performance with additional modules. The first thing to check is that you have one or more spare slots available and to compare the total installed RAM with what is recommended for your operating system.

Table 8.01 Memory requirements for Windows

Version	Minimum	Recommended
XP Home/Professional	128MB	256MB
Vista	512MB	1GB

The recommended figures are, in reality, the minimum you will need to obtain anything like reasonable performance, and if you are planning on running any memory-intensive applications like sound or video editing then doubling the recommended (or more) RAM will be a worthwhile investment.

Total installed RAM can be found by right-clicking on (My) Computer and looking at its Properties. The number of empty RAM slots can be determined by taking the lid or side panel off the system and having a look.

The easiest way to find what types of RAM are available for your system is to visit memory manufacturers' websites and look it up. Crucial – one of the big manufacturers – has a free download program which will detect the type and amount of installed RAM and recommend (and give you a price for) upgrade options.

Figure 8.01 shows a typical Dual Inline Memory Module (DIMM). This type has notches in the face which fit into the motherboard slot so that it will only go in the right way around.

Having decided on the memory upgrade, and acquired it, you are ready to install. To fit the new RAM stick(s) you need access to the interior of the PC.

1 Power down the PC, disconnect from the mains power supply, and remove the case, cover or side panel. Don't forget to touch bare metal or use a wrist strap before you touch any of the internal components.

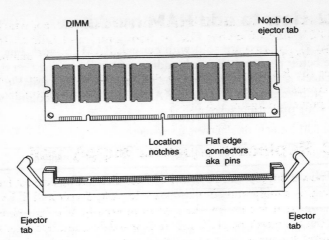

DIMM

Notch for
ejector tab

Location
notches

Flat edge
connectors
aka pins

Ejector
tab

Ejector
tab

Figure 8.01

2 If it is a tower case lay it on its side so that the motherboard is parallel to your work surface.

3 Remove the new RAM module from its packaging. **Do not touch** the connector edges with your fingers.

4 Flip back the ejector tabs on the motherboard RAM slot.

5 Check that the module is the right way round for the slot. (The notches on the underside ensure it will only fit one way.)

6 Push the module down into the slot, vertically, until the ejector tabs click into place, then push them gently to make sure that they are fully engaged.

7 To fit the module you will have to push it firmly into place, but you should not use excessive force. As with most hardware jobs, if you have to force it, you are probably doing it wrong – wrong orientation of the component with the slot or socket being the commonest error.

8 Repeat the steps for any other RAM modules. When you have finished, reconnect the power and start up the PC to check that the new memory is in place and working. All being well, the PC will beep once and boot to the operating system where you can verify that your new RAM is recognized by the system – right-clicking on *(My) Computer* will report the total installed memory.

If the PC emits a series of beeps (not just a single beep, which is the PC's way of saying OK, at boot time) and fails to start properly, power down and reseat the memory and try again.

Once the RAM is in place and working, power down, replace the covers or panels which you removed in order to gain access, and power up again. Job done!

8.3 Replacing a power supply unit

The power supply unit in your PC takes alternating current from the mains supply and converts it to 12 volt, 5 volt and 3.3 volt direct current for use by the system internally. If a PSU simply dies the PC won't work. If it is failing – delivering less than the required voltage – you may experience boot time failures. In this situation the PC will start to boot, then fail. Repeating the attempt may secure a successful boot and the machine will run, but there will be problems next boot time. To check the output of the power supply, use a multimeter on its output lines. You should see readings of 12 volts (yellow), 5 volts (red), 3.3 volts (orange). As little as one-tenth of a volt below the required voltage can be enough to cause problems.

As is frequently the case, the easiest solution is to replace like with like, though you may want to increase the wattage rating of the new PSU if the old one is rated lower than (say) 400 watts. Figure 8.02 shows an ATX Power Supply Unit.

To replace a PSU:

1 Power down the PC, disconnect from the mains supply, and remove the case, cover or side panel.

2 Disconnect the power lines from the various drives and the motherboard.

3 Turn the PC so that you are looking at the back of the case.

4 Remove the screws (usually four) which hold the PSU in place.

5 Remove the old PSU.

6 Put the new PSU in place and fix it with the screws you saved from the old unit.

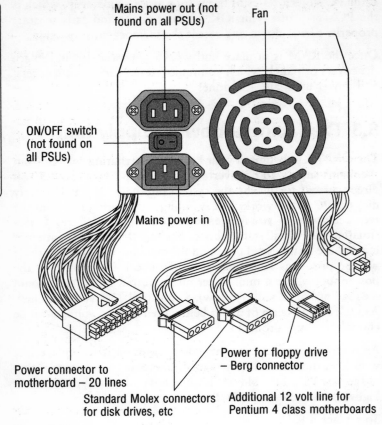

Mains power out (not
found on all PSUs)

Fan

ON/OFF switch
(not found on
all PSUs)

Mains power in

Power connector to
motherboard – 20 lines

Power for floppy drive
– Berg connector

Standard Molex connectors
for disk drives, etc

Additional 12 volt line for
Pentium 4 class motherboards

Figure 8.02

7 Connect output lines to the motherboard and the drives.

8 Power up and test, then power down and replace the covers.

Note: the connector to the motherboard is keyed so that it will
only fit one way, and the Molex connectors (4 pins) have two
bevelled edges so that they can only be fitted the right way round
in the disk drives. Any drive can take its power from any
connector of the appropriate type.

Be careful, too, when reconnecting the floppy drive. It is possible,
but difficult, to force the power connector on upside down, and
doing this will burn out the drive.

8.4 How to add a second hard disk

Adding a second hard disk drive increases your storage capacity in a very cost-effective way. Your operating system and programs remain in place on your primary drive (the C: drive) and – after fitting – your new drive is available for additional storage.

Most PCs are equipped with a single hard disk drive which is either a serial or parallel ATA type. Serial ATA uses a small flat 7-pin data connector and a 15-pin power cable (see Figure 7.04).

Parallel ATA uses a 40-pin connector and an 80-line ribbon cable for data, and a standard Molex connector for power. Figure 8.03 shows a drive of this type.

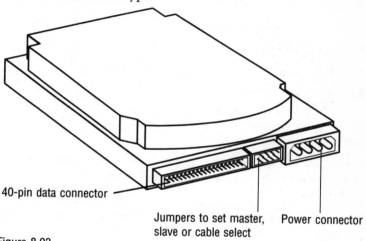

40-pin data connector

Jumpers to set master, slave or cable select

Power connector

Figure 8.03

While it is possible to mix drive types on the same system it is best to use similar types. If your first drive is serial, use a serial drive for the second drive: if the primary is a parallel drive then use a parallel drive for the second drive.

Masters, slaves and jumper settings

Unlike the more modern Serial ATA (SATA) drives, parallel ATA drives like the one in Figure 8.03, and CD/DVD drives, require you to set jumpers to identify the drive as 'master' or 'slave'.

Most motherboards have two 40-pin connectors for ATA drives (see *Disk drive controllers*, page 97) and each controller supports two devices referred to as master and slave. This is needed to distinguish the drives which are sharing a controller and a cable. To do this you set a jumper on the back (or sometimes the underside) of the drive. Jumper settings are usually indicated by a label on the drive. For each cable, set one drive as master and the other as slave using the jumpers as shown in Figure 8.03.

An alternative to this method is to use the cable-select (CS) option. Systems which use cable-select have colour coded connectors on the data cable. To set up a pair of drives using this method, set the jumpers on both drives to the CS option and attach them to the data cable. The colour coding on the cable works like this:

*   Blue connects to the motherboard

*   Grey connects to the slave drive

*   Black connects to the master drive.

By convention, the Windows operating system is usually on the master drive on the primary controller (drive C:) – this was a requirement in earlier versions of Windows and has remained as a (rather sensible) convention.

Regardless of the drive type, it will need to be fixed in the case and attached to both power and data cables.

Power down the PC, disconnect it from the mains and remove the cover or side panel to access the inside of the machine. Set jumpers, where necessary, fit the new drive in a spare bay and connect the power and data cables. Reconnect the machine to the power – don't put the lid or side panel back yet, you may have to adjust or correct something if you make a mistake. If you do get it wrong – it's quite easy to set a jumper incorrectly – they system won't work, but you won't do any damage. Just start again and experiment until you get it right. Something to watch out for, particularly with older drives, is different jumper settings for standalone master and master with slave present.

With your new drive in place, reboot the machine. If you have set the jumpers correctly and connected the data and power cables as required, Windows will find the new drive when you reboot.

The next job is to prepare it for use. You will need Administrator privileges for this. Open the **Control Panel** and select **Administrative Tools**, then **Computer Management**, and at its window select **Disk Management**. You will see something like Figure 8.04.

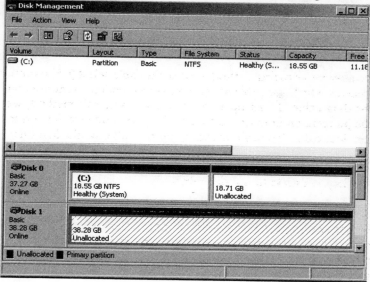

Figure 8.04

The figure shows two hard disks on a Windows XP Professional system. The C: drive is on Disk 0 along with some unallocated space on that drive: the new drive is Disk 1 which, in this instance, has 38.28Gb of 'Unallocated' space. To prepare the disk for use you need to do two things: partition it, and then format it.

1 To create a new partition, right-click on Disk 1 and select the **New Partition** option as in Figure 8.05

Figure 8.05

2 At this point you may make one or more partitions on your new disk prior to formatting them. In this example there is

only one partition which fills the whole of the new disk, but you are not necessarily restricted to this.

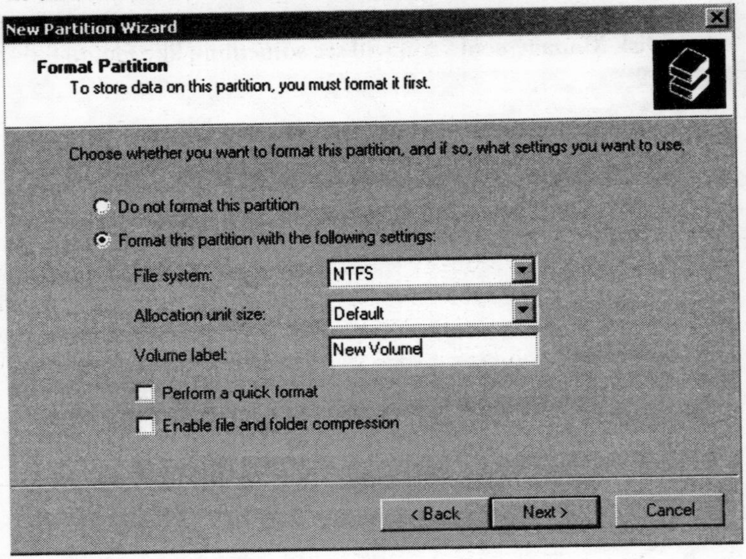

New Partition Wizard ✕

Format Partition
To store data on this partition, you must format it first.

Choose whether you want to format this partition, and if so, what settings you want to use.

○ Do not format this partition

◉ Format this partition with the following settings:

File system:	NTFS
Allocation unit size:	Default
Volume label:	New Volume

☐ Perform a quick format

☐ Enable file and folder compression

< Back   Next >   Cancel

Figure 8.06

3 Accept the default settings from the Wizard and click **Next**. The Wizard will start to format the new drive.

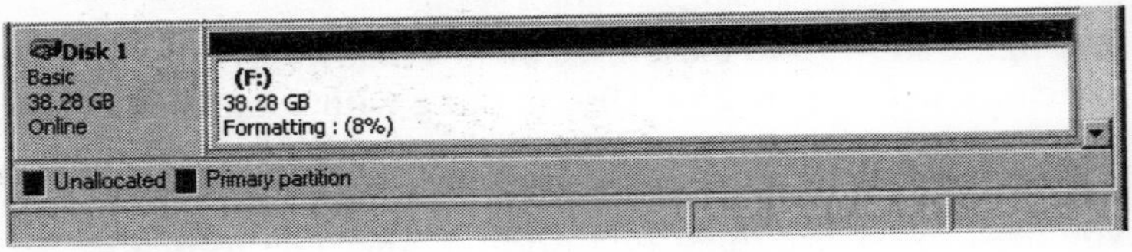

Disk 1
Basic
38.28 GB
Online

(F:)
38.28 GB
Formatting : (8%)

■ Unallocated ■ Primary partition

Figure 8.07

4 Note the new drive letter and the progress report of the formatting process. This will take several minutes and needs no further user input – an ideal time for a cup of tea or coffee!

5 When the Wizard has completed, close it down. Navigate to (My) Computer and check that the new drive is in place.

 New Volume (F:)

Figure 8.08

6 Right-click on the drive icon, select **Properties** and give the new drive a more meaningful name such as **Data Disk**.

Your new disk is now ready to use. Power down, check that all cabling is neatly arranged and nothing is snagging, replace the cover or side panel, put the machine back in its proper place and turn it on. Finally, congratulate yourself on a job well done!

8.5 How to add or replace a CD or DVD drive

Adding or replacing a CD or DVD drive is a similar undertaking to fitting a second hard disk, but is easier to do because the new drive does not need to be partitioned or formatted. (Note: hard disks are ATA devices, CD/DVDs are ATAPI devices, though the distinction is not important for our present practical purposes.)

Figure 8.09 shows the back of a typical CD/DVD drive.

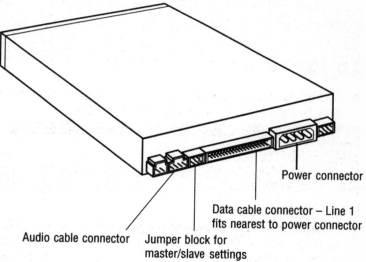

Power connector

Data cable connector – Line 1 fits nearest to power connector

Audio cable connector   Jumper block for master/slave settings

Figure 8.09

1 Power down the PC, disconnect from the mains power supply, and remove the case, cover or side panel.

2 If you are replacing an old drive, disconnect the cables from the back of the drive, remove the screws that hold it in place (usually 2 on each side) and slide it out of the front of the

case. Note the position of the jumper which sets master or slave and use the same jumper setting on the new drive.

3   Slide the drive into place, attach cables as for the old drive.

4   Fix in place with the screws saved from the old drive.

5   Turn on and test before powering down again and replacing the cover or side panel.

If, rather than replacing a CD or DVD drive, you are adding one, the procedure is fundamentally similar. The easiest way is to add the second drive to the spare connector on the data cable attached to the first. Having opened the PC case:

1   Remove the cover from the drive bay on the front of the PC. You may also have to break out a small metal internal cover.

2   Check the jumper setting on the existing drive and set the jumper on the new drive to be the opposite (so that you end up with one master and one slave on the same cable).

8.6 How to add a tape drive

Tape drives are most commonly used to back up server machines in the commercial world where there may be a lot of data which changes rapidly. Not many home users will need a tape drive, but if you are one of the few, then it's really much the same as fitting a CD/DVD drive. Choose a drive which uses the standard 40-pin ATA style connector, choose appropriate jumper settings as for a CD/DVD drive and fit it in the case.

8.7 How to fit a floppy drive

Many modern PCs are sold without a floppy drive which can be inconvenient for some maintenance jobs. There are external floppy drives available, but you can fit an internal one easily for a few pounds as long as you have a floppy controller on the motherboard and a 3½-inch bay on the front of the case. Fitting a floppy drive means that you will have a drive for running diagnostic programs or for copying small files to another PC.

The first thing to do is to check that you have a drive bay available and that there is a floppy controller on the motherboard. Remove the side panel or cover of the PC and check. The floppy controller on the motherboard has 34 pins in two rows and looks like a smaller version of the hard disk controllers.

You will need a floppy drive and a floppy drive cable. These are normally quite cheap to buy. They are also very easy to fit.

To fit your new floppy drive:

1 Power down the PC, disconnect from the mains supply and remove the cover. The drive bay at the front of the case will have a plastic cover plate: this can be pushed out from behind. If there is a metal cover behind it then this too must be removed by breaking it. It is made of a soft alloy and is usually perforated to make it easy to break out. It may not feel right, but it is intended to be broken and removed.

2 Slide the new floppy drive into the bay, and line up the front of the drive with the front of the case. Inside the case, the drive will be sitting in a metal cage with fixing points on either side. There are usually two screw holes on each side of the drive itself. Fit the screws in the sides of the drive so that it is held in place. Don't overtighten them.

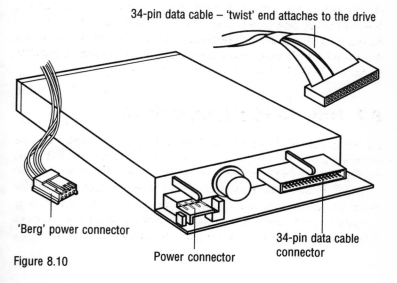

34-pin data cable – 'twist' end attaches to the drive

'Berg' power connector

Power connector

34-pin data cable connector

Figure 8.10

3   After you have double-checked that the drive is properly aligned with the front of the case, fit the data cable.

Figure 8.10 shows a floppy disk drive and data cable. There are two connectors fairly close to one another at the drive end of the cable (so that you can fit two floppy drives if you want to) – the other end of the cable fits on the motherboard.

A floppy cable has 34 connectors for the 34 pins on the drive. Cables and drives are usually keyed so that they can only be connected correctly. Where there isn't a keying system, the coloured stripe on the edge of the cable indicates line 1. Pin 1 on the drive is probably marked, though it is not always easy to see.

There is a twist in the cable between the end connectors. The last connector – the one after the twist – is the one you should connect to the floppy drive. This ensures that the new drive will appear on the system as Drive A:. (The other connector – the one before the twist – is for drive B: on a twin floppy machine.)

4   Connect the other end of the data cable to the controller on the motherboard. Where the controller and the cable are keyed, the cable can only be fitted correctly, otherwise the coloured stripe on the cable should correspond with pin 1 on the controller.

5   Finally, fit the power connector to the floppy drive. There is really only one way that this will fit, but it is just about possible to force it on the wrong way. If you do this you will damage your new drive. The data cable is not so critical.

6   With the new drive in place, reconnect the PC and turn it on. Watch the light on the new floppy drive. If it has been fitted correctly the light will flash briefly as the system starts up, and then go out. If the drive light remains permanently on, then the data cable is fitted back to front (i.e. pin 1 on the drive is connected to line 34 on the cable). If this happens, you won't have damaged the drive – power down and reverse the orientation of the cable on the drive and try again.

7   If, at this stage, nothing at all is happening, it may be that the new drive has to be enabled in CMOS/BIOS. Refer to the *How to access the BIOS/CMOS settings* section of Chapter 6 if you are in doubt about this.

8 The final test, with the PC running, is to put a floppy disk in the drive and test that the system can read and write to it. When you are satisfied that all is well, power down the PC, disconnect from the mains and replace the cover/side panel, then reconnect and reboot.

8.8 How to fit a PCI expansion card

The Peripheral Component Interconnect (PCI) expansion slot is the most widely used general purpose expansion slot for adding hardware devices to your PC. Network Interface Cards (NICs), internal modems, sound cards, additional USB or Fire wire ports can all be added to your system through the PCI slots. A more modern variant of PCI is the PCI-X slot (PCI eXtended) – this is a higher speed development of the standard PCI slot and is a different length to the standard PCI connector.

Provided the expansion card and the slot match, the procedure for fitting a new PCI card is the same for all types and devices:

1 Power down.

2 Fit the card.

3 Power up.

4 Install any necessary drivers.

5 Reboot the PC and test.

Modern Windows versions support most of the common hardware expansion cards out of the box – that is, the operating system ships with the necessary software drivers. However, if there are drivers provided by the manufacturer with the card, these may be more up-to-date and you may wish to use these, or download the newest drivers from the manufacturer's website.

If you are going to use the manufacturer's own drivers, read the fitting/installation instructions first. Some devices require you to install drivers before fitting the expansion card.

If your device plugs and plays (and most devices these days do) then you can either choose the Have Disk option to install the manufacturer's drivers, or install the drivers provided by Windows with a view to updating them later.

To update drivers for a device, navigate to Device Manager, select the device in question, right-click and select Update Driver. This launches a Wizard which allows you to search both local drives and the Internet for drivers.

8.9 How to fit an AGP graphics card

Fitting an AGP graphics card is much the same as fitting a PCI card. Check that the card is the right size and type for the slot on your motherboard, power down, fit the card, power up and test.

By default – even without additional drivers – your new graphics card will give you some sort of output – usually a screen resolution of 800 × 600 – which is sufficient for you to install the full set of drivers for the card.

Your new card will be accompanied by a CD containing the manufacturer's drivers. Read the instructions, then install the drivers. Reboot the PC if necessary and configure your graphics settings. To do this, right-click on a blank area of the Desktop, select Properties and choose the Settings tab. Here you can set the screen resolution, number of colours, etc. You can also use the Advanced option to change other settings such as the monitor refresh rate. Be careful with this because although a rate that is too low can cause eye strain, setting it too high can permanently damage the monitor. (It is rare that a software setting can damage hardware, but this is the exception that proves the rule.)

8.10 How to replace a motherboard

Replacing a motherboard is probably the most ambitious hardware task that you are likely to tackle. To keep things simple, I shall assume that you are simply replacing like with like – i.e. the same make and model.

If you want to upgrade to a different motherboard, there are many considerations about compatibility with your other components, and you may well have to reinstall the operating system. This is of course possible, but is beyond the scope of this book. As it is, even replacing like with like is close to rebuilding the whole system.

Once you have identified your motherboard and bought the replacement you are ready to begin. Allow plenty of time for this and make sure that you have space to lay things out, containers for screws, pen and paper and, if possible, a digital camera.

1 Begin by disconnecting the PC and removing the side panel. Take a close look at the layout of the internal components and make notes of the position of various cables – particularly the small cables that attach to the LEDs on the front of the case. A couple of photographs of the inside of the case will be very useful at this point. Take them and make sure that you can access them or print them for future reference.

2 There is no set order for removing the components from the case, though it's probably easier to remove the cables first. As each component is removed place it somewhere safe, away from the immediate work area.

3 Remove all of the expansion cards, but leave the CPU chip and RAM modules in place. Remove the fixing screws that hold the motherboard in place and lift it out. (This might be a good time to clean out some of the dust!)

4 In the now empty case you will see some brass fixing points for the motherboard. These are known as posts or standoffs. Their purpose is to provide fixing points for the motherboard which will hold it in place without touching the case.

5 Remove the new motherboard from its anti-static packaging and put it in the case, lining it up with the standoffs. Make sure that the external ports line up with the openings in the back of the case. (A second pair of hands at this stage can be very useful!) With everything lined up, screw the motherboard to the standoffs, making sure that the screws are tight, but not using excessive force.

With the new motherboard in place, it's time to check the job. This is a two-stage process. We start with a 'bare bones build'.

1 Remove the heat sink and fan from the old processor. The fan will unscrew, and the heat sink is normally held in place by a clip. The CPU itself is held in place by a lever which is part of the CPU socket. (This is known as a *Zero Insertion*

Force or ZIF socket and the lever as a ZIF lever.) Pull the ZIF lever until it is vertical and remove the chip. Put it in the ZIF socket on the new motherboard – it will only fit one way. If the processor is properly oriented and seated, the ZIF arm will drop down easily and fix the CPU in place.

2   Fit the heat sink on the top of the newly installed CPU and fix the fan. Make sure that the power lead to the fan is connected to the motherboard and that it is the right way round.

3   Transfer the RAM modules to the new motherboard. Connect the power supply to the motherboard and reconnect the small wires from it to the front of the case. Make sure that the case speaker is reconnected.

4   Now, in this half-assembled state, connect the system to the mains power and turn it on. Make sure that the CPU fan works as soon as the system is powered up and if it does not **switch off immediately** and fix it.

5   Once you are sure that the CPU fan is working, allow the PC to go through the boot sequence. If the motherboard is properly installed and the CPU and RAM are correctly installed the machine will start to boot. The case speaker will emit a lot of rapid beeps – this is the machine complaining that it can't find its keyboard, disk drives, etc. This is good news – if it's whingeing it's working! You have a successful bare bones build. If it's not working, then there are only a handful of components to check – that's the point of the bare bones build – to keep things simple. It's easier to debug a handful of components than a whole system!

6   With the basic build in place and working, you can replace the disk drives and other components. With a graphics card and monitor in place you will get visual output. Replacing the hard drive will give you an operating system, and so on until you have a fully rebuilt working system.

7   When you have finished your rebuild, replace all covers and panels, reinstate the machine to its proper place in the household and test everything you can think of.

Summary

This chapter has looked at some of the more common tasks which you may want to carry out in order to replace or upgrade common hardware components on a typical home system. Some of the tasks – such as fitting additional RAM – are relatively straightforward; others, like replacing a motherboard are quite ambitious. One of the decisions that you have to make in home PC maintenance is whether a particular job is within your abilities or whether to call an outside technician. If you can do it yourself – fine. If you call in an outside techie, at least you know what is involved and you should be able to agree a fair price for the work.

09 preventive maintenance

In this chapter you will learn:

- how to organize your maintenance schedule

- how to work without damaging the equipment

- how to dispose of old components legally and safely

9.1 A maintenance schedule

Preventive maintenance and cleaning are tedious but necessary if you want to keep your system running efficiently, and a regular maintenance schedule can save you time and money on maintenance and repair bills.

The key to effective maintenance is a regular pattern of work. Some tasks should be done daily, some weekly, some occasionally.

Daily

♦ **Virus scan.** Your virus scanner should have the capability of running at a pre-set time each day. If you leave your system permanently on, you can schedule this for the small hours of the morning. Don't forget that the scanner needs to update its 'definitions' files, so schedule the update to run just before the scan. There's more on viruses in Chapter 16, *Viruses and other malware.*

♦ **Spyware scan.** This complements the virus scan and ideally, it should be done immediately before or after the virus scan. More in Chapter 16.

♦ **Backup.** It is prudent to back up your data daily. The minimum you should do is to back up data which has been modified (a differential backup) with a full data backup once a week. Chapter 6, *Backup strategies* has more on this.

Weekly

♦ **Full data backup,** preferably to a rotating disk (or tape) set.

♦ **Defragment** the hard disk (see Chapter 1).

♦ Run the **Disk Cleanup** Wizard (see Chapter 1).

Monthly

♦ Clean **optical drives** – CDROM/DVD – with a cleaner disk.

♦ **Archive backup** of data – store away from the PC.

♦ **Mouse** – if you are still using a 'ball' mouse, clean the rollers by scraping gently with a toothpick or similar.

- **Monitor** – power down and clean the screen with a soft cloth or an anti-static wipe.

- Check the **keyboard** for sticky keys – clean with canned air if necessary.

On failure

- **Floppy disk drive.** The cleaning disk which you can use for cleaning floppy drives is mildly abrasive, so it should only be used sparingly to avoid long-term cumulative damage to the drive.

Yearly

- **Case.** Open the case. Remove dust deposits by brushing gently with a natural bristle brush, then blow out with canned air, or use a special PC vacuum cleaner.

- Adaptor **cards, cables** and removable **components** – clean contacts and reseat.

Ongoing/as required

- **CMOS** – record and/or backup CMOS settings.

- **System** – maintain a record of hardware, software and settings of the system. Don't forget your email account settings, dialup numbers and passwords. Note all changes in a system notebook – that's 'notebook' in the old fashioned sense of a pen and paper record – it doesn't need mains power, batteries, or disk storage and there's a lot to be said for that!

9.2 Cleaning products and tools

Commonly used products and tools include:

- **Canned air.** Use this for blowing dust from awkward corners. Most PC shops sell it.

- **Natural fibre brushes.** A small paint brush or a pastry brush is ideal. Make sure, though, that it has natural bristles as some man-made fibres can generate static electricity which could damage components.

- **Antistatic wipes.** These are usually individually wrapped. They can be bought from most PC shops.

- **Denatured alcohol.** This can simply be a bottle of meths or surgical spirit which you can buy from a hardware shop or pharmacy. Alcohol cuts through grease very effectively and evaporates quickly.

- **Mild detergent solution.** Tap water with a squirt of washing-up liquid is a very good cleaning solution, especially for the outside of the case, etc. It needs to be used with care, of course, as water and electricity can be a hazardous combination. Don't apply the solution directly, use a dampened cloth and use sparingly.

- **Cleaning disks.** The disks which you use on a floppy drive are mildly abrasive and should be used with restraint. The cleaning disks/kits which you can use for CD or DVD drives are not generally abrasive and can be used as necessary or monthly as a routine preventive measure.

- **Cotton buds.** These are useful for general purpose cleaning. They can be used in conjunction with canned air and a natural bristle brush for mechanical removal of dirt and debris from awkward corners. They can also be dipped in alcohol for liquid cleaning where necessary.

- **Non-static vacuum cleaners.** These are small cleaners – often pistol grip in shape – which are intended for use with PCs. They need to be used with care as there is the possibility of damaging or dislodging components.

Safety note

Before using any product on your PC, check that it is suitable for its intended use. For instance, if you plan on cleaning the case with a detergent solution or alcohol, apply it to a small area that is usually out of sight to check that it's okay.

In terms of Health and Safety law in the UK, there are regulations under the *Control of Substances Hazardous to Health* (COSHH) regulations, and in the US all such products have a *Material Safety Data Sheet* (MSDS). You can check the nature of any product by searching on the Internet.

9.3 Cleaning the outside of the case

Power down and 'wash' with a cloth that has been dipped in mild detergent solution and wrung out. Allow the cleaned surfaces to dry fully before reconnecting the power. For a really good job, you can follow detergent cleaning with a rub down with a cloth that has been moistened with alcohol. Again, allow the cleaned surface to dry fully before reconnecting the power.

Cleaning monitors

LCD – flat panel – monitors can be cleaned with a glass cleaner and a lint-free cloth. Don't spray the cleaner directly on to the screen, but apply a small amount to the cloth, then wipe the surface with it. LCD screens are easily scratched, so you should work gently. Be careful not to leave any excess on the screen and allow half an hour or so before powering up again.

Cathode ray tube (CRT) monitors – the ones that look like television sets – need to be treated with care. Even when they are turned off they contain very high voltages. Always disconnect the monitor before working on it and never wear a wrist strap or even metal jewellery that could come into contact with it.

A simple soap-and-water solution can be used for cleaning the outside of the case and the screen itself. Don't use excessive amounts of the solution: dip the cleaning cloth in it, then wring out until it is damp but has no excess moisture. Clean the monitor and dry it with a clean cloth before powering up. Don't use commercial cleaners or aerosol sprays other than those specifically designed for use with monitors.

With either type of monitor, power up when you have finished and the screen is dry, then check that any controls for brightness, alignment, etc. are okay. It's quite easy to knock a control accidentally during cleaning and to lose the 'picture' as a result.

9.4 Cleaning inside the case

Dust is an ever present problem with computer systems. The components generate static charges as a by-product of their operation, and the various cooling fans draw air (and dust) into the case. Over time, the accumulation of dust can be sufficient to cause overheating, so an annual spring clean of the interior of the case can be a useful investment of your time.

As with all work on the inside of the system box, power down and disconnect from the mains before removing the covers or side panels.

The first line of defence against accumulated dust is a small paint brush, or a pastry brush, with natural bristles which will not induce static in the components to which it is applied. Simply use the brush to dislodge accumulated dust – particularly on the CPU heat sink/fan assembly and the power supply fan. The loosened dust can be blown away using canned air or removed with a non-static vacuum cleaner.

While you have the case open, it is a good time to check that all of the fans rotate freely and are properly connected to the power connectors on the motherboard – it's quite easy to dislodge connection during the cleaning process. This is also a good time to replace any missing covers from unused expansion slots. This will help to optimize the airflow in the case and to keep atmospheric dust out.

Before replacing the cover or side panel, connect the machine to the mains and power up. Check that all fans – particularly the CPU fan – are working. A non-functioning CPU fan will cause the chip to overheat and the system will lock up in under a minute. Longer than a minute is sufficient to cause permanent damage so this is a check worth making.

Cleaning contacts and connections

This is not really necessary where a system is functioning properly, but some people like to clean and reseat internal components as part of their annual maintenance. If components have been handled and fitted properly – that is, contacts and edge connectors have never been touched by hand – then there is not likely to be any corrosion or oxidation to the surface.

If you do find it necessary to clean edge connectors on expansion cards or memory modules, then remove the module and use a very fine emery cloth or a specialist electrical contact cleaner spray. The easiest method is to use a pencil eraser to brush the contacts. When doing this, always work from the inner to the outer edge of the module to avoid peeling back the edge connectors.

Other internal components which fit into slots or sockets on the motherboard may work themselves loose over time. The repeated cycle of heating and cooling causes repeated expansions and contractions of the components which can cause them to work loose in their sockets – a phenomenon known as 'chip creep'. As a preventive measure, it may be prudent to remove and reseat any such components to establish a fresh electrical contact.

9.5 Cleaning removable media devices

Removable drives such as tape drives, floppy drives, CDs, DVDs, etc. are open to the air, and the media themselves are physically handled. This means that they can collect dust and finger grease which can be transferred from the disk to the drive heads. An indirect form of preventive maintenance, then, is to exercise care when handling removable media.

Magnetic media, floppy disks and tapes, etc., can easily be corrupted if they are stored close to strong magnetic fields, so you should avoid storing them near anything with an electric motor – like a vacuum cleaner – or anything with strong electro-magnetic fields such as CRT monitors or speakers.

When it comes to cleaning drives themselves, there are two approaches: removal and manual cleaning or using cleaning tapes or disks. Generally speaking, floppy drives are now so cheap that it may be cost-effective to replace then rather than spend time on cleaning them, though cleaning kits are available.

Optical drives – CD and DVD – as well as tape drives may be removed, stripped down and cleaned with alcohol and a lint-free cloth. A cotton bud dipped in meths is an easy way to clean a lens. As an alternative, there are cleaning disks and kits available for most drive types. Optical media are mechanically 'swept' clean by brush heads mounted on a cleaning disk which passes over the laser lens. This is a non-destructive process. Cleaners for magnetic media are generally mildly abrasive so, whilst they are effective at removing the build up of contaminants on the drive heads, excessive use can shorten the life of the drive.

Ventilation, dust and moisture control

Fortunately, PCs do best in the same sort of conditions that most of us find comfortable: not too hot, not too cold, moderate humidity and no sources of dust. Most domestic users will have no problems, but air conditioning systems can sometimes lower humidity to sub-optimal levels.

When you are carrying out preventive maintenance inside the case, look out for unusual patterns in the (inevitable) build up of dust in the case as these may indicate missing expansion slot covers or cracks in the case.

Surge suppressors

Mains electrical supplies are subject to interruptions, voltage 'sags' and occasional 'spikes'. In commerce and industry, key machines are often protected by various technologies such as line conditioners and uninterruptible power supplies. For most home users, these technologies are disproportionate and expensive. However, a simple surge suppressor costs only a few pounds and will provide basic protection against power surges in the mains supply which could otherwise damage your system. If you don't have a surge suppressor – buy one!

9.7 Safe disposal of old equipment

Nearly everything inside a computer seems to be toxic and there are increasing levels of concern by government and local authorities about safe disposal. Before disposing of any piece of equipment it is wise to enquire about current legal requirements for the country, county or state where you live.

Batteries contain many toxic substances and need to be disposed of through a recognized disposal facility. They should never be incinerated or thrown out with household rubbish. Batteries which are damaged, or which leak, present a hazard to anyone handling them – be especially careful not to get electrolyte in your eyes.

Monitors – particularly CRT monitors – contain many toxic substances and may contain potentially lethal voltages even when they have been turned off for some time. They are subject to ever-tightening disposal regulations and you should find a specialist disposal facility.

Toner cartridges, refill kits and old ink jet cartridges may also need special disposal. However, many of these items are refillable and/or recyclable. Empty laser toner cartridges may even be saleable.

If you are in any doubt about the nature of any component or substance that you have to dispose of, then a search of the Internet for the UK *Control of Substances Hazardous to Health* (COSHH) regulations or the US counterpart *Material Safety Data Sheet* (MSDS) will give an indication of what is appropriate and/or legally required.

Summary

This chapter has looked at preventive maintenance procedures which will extend the life and reliability of your system. It is unglamorous stuff – the sort of thing you can generally put off until next week – but if you make the effort, and adopt a systematic approach to preventive maintenance, it will save you time and money in the long run. You know it makes sense!

10

peripheral devices

In this chapter you will learn:

- about the main external ports

- about the cables and connectors associated with each port type

- how to install device drivers

10.1 Ports

From the earliest days of the PC, systems have been built to be extensible by attaching additional components to the expansion slots *inside* the case and attaching peripheral devices – printers, scanners, cameras, etc. – to the PC's external ports.

Ports are integrated into the system through their connection to the motherboard. This may be an attachment through an expansion card in a slot, or it may be an 'on-board' port, that is, directly connected to or built into the motherboard at the time of manufacture.

Whether they are on-board or on expansion cards, the main PC ports provide a means of connecting external – or peripheral devices. Some of them have only one purpose – *dedicated* ports such as VGA or DVI for graphics output – or they may be general-purpose ports which allow the connection of any device which has the appropriate interface. Figure 10.01 shows the common ports that you might expect to see at the back of a PC.

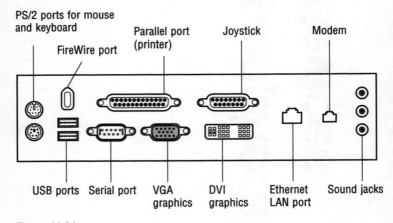

Figure 10.01

Some of these ports – particularly USB and FireWire – are often fitted to the front of the case on modern PCs. There are even instances of USB ports built into the side of a Flat Panel monitor. However, their location does not dictate their use.

10.2 Dedicated ports

Keyboard and mouse (PS/2s)

The small round connectors for the keyboard and mouse are known as PS/2s after the IBM PC model of that name. More often that not, these days, they are colour coded: purple for the keyboard and green for the mouse. This is not an official standard – just a convention that has emerged in recent years. If your connectors are not colour coded there will usually be some indication on the case of which is which. You need to exercise care when reconnecting these. If you plug the keyboard into the mouse port (and vice versa) and attempt to reboot the PC you won't do any damage, but you may find that it will refuse to start up at all. If you do get this wrong, power down before putting it right. PS/2 connectors are not 'hot swappable'.

Graphics – VGA and DVI

The Video Graphics Array (VGA) connector is still the one most frequently used for a monitor. It has 15 pins in three rows.

The Digital Video Interface (DVI) connector has 29 pins: 24 of these are used for power and digital signals, and five for analog signals. It is sometimes referred to as a '24+5 DVI Connector'. Adaptors are available so that you can attach a VGA connector to a DVI port and vice versa.

Attaching a monitor is really as simple as plugging it into the graphics port, providing it with power and booting the PC. If it is a new monitor, Windows will detect it at boot time and you may be prompted for drivers from the manufacturer's CD.

Once the drivers are installed you may need to tweak a few settings. There are usually some controls – buttons, most likely – on the front of the monitor which can be used to change the position of the picture, its height, brightness, contrast and so on. These controls will be specific to your monitor so you should consult the manual or instructions which came with it. Failing that, just sit and experiment, making notes if necessary, until you obtain the display characteristics you want.

Having set the monitor to your liking through hardware, you may want to further fine-tune it through the operating system. Use the Display applet in the Control Panel or right-click on an empty piece of your Desktop and select Properties. Whichever route you choose, you will see something like Figure 10.02.

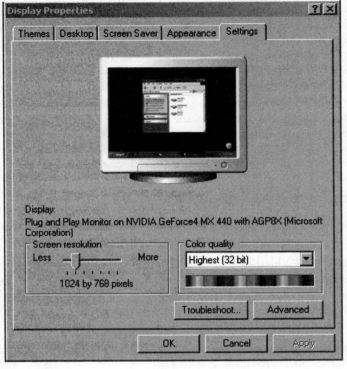

Figure 10.02

Experiment until you find resolution and colour quality settings which suit you. LCD (Flat Panel) monitors are generally designed to work at one optimal resolution. CRT monitors are more flexible in this respect. If you click **Advanced** and select the **Monitor** tab you can change the refresh rate of the monitor. This is the frequency with which it redraws the lines which make up the display. If it is set too low it can cause eyestrain; if it is set too high you can damage the monitor. Most people find a refresh rate in the range 75Hz to 85Hz comfortable to work with.

Modem (internal)

The modem port at the back of your system is known as an RJ-11 which is the United States' standard telephone connector. In the UK, you will need a modem cable with an RJ-11 at the PC end and a standard BT connector at the other. If the cable has RJ-11s at both ends, you can use an adaptor at the phone end.

Configuring a modem – whether internal or external – may require you to provide software drivers. You will also need to enter some information from your Internet Service Provider (ISP) such as the dialup phone number, your user name and password. Installing and configuring a modem is a topic in Chapter 15, *The Internet and email.*

Network: RJ-45

The RJ-45 is similar in appearance to the RJ-11 though it is slightly larger. It is the most commonly used network connector. It may be built into the motherboard or it may have been added through an expansion card.

If you have installed a new Network Interface Card (NIC) or have reinstalled Windows you may have to provide drivers for it. Most hardware of this type will plug and play – just follow the instructions on the screen. If it doesn't plug and play run the Add New Hardware Wizard which you can access through the Control Panel.

Configuring the network connection – IP addressing, etc. – is covered in Chapter 17, *Home networking.*

10.3 General-purpose ports

Parallel ports

The parallel port has been a part of every PC from the very earliest days. It is 'D' shaped in section and has 25 pins and data lines. Originally it only allowed data to pass in one direction: from the PC to the attached device. Since it was mainly used for attaching a printer to the PC it is often referred to as a printer port or PRN or LPT1.

Modern systems are more demanding than the early PCs. These days we expect a printer to be able to send back error or status messages such as 'out of paper', or to be able to run diagnostics or print-head cleaning and alignment utilities. We may also want to connect a device such as a scanner where the data flow is predominantly *to* (rather than *from*) the PC.

If you have problems with a printer which suggest that it is not communicating with the PC it may be that the printer port needs to be reconfigured in the CMOS Setup. To do this:

1 Reboot the PC and enter the **Setup** utility.

2 If there is a setting for the printer port (or PRN or LPT1) and it reads **SPP** then it is configured as a Standard Parallel Port. Change this to **EPP** (Enhanced Parallel Port) or **ECP** (Enhanced Capabilities Port).

3 Save your changes, exit from the setup screen and try again.

Note that the highest specification port type (ECP) may require a special cable to use all of its facilities. As with so many things with a PC, experiment until you find something that works for you. (There's more about CMOS/BIOS settings in Chapter 6.)

Serial ports

Serial ports have also been part of the PC since the earliest days. By modern standards, they are slow, but they are still sometimes used. Like the parallel port they are 'D' shaped in section. Unlike the parallel port they are invariably male. The commonest size for a serial port is nine pins, though the older 25-pin version is still sometimes used. Serial ports are also referred to as RS-232 ports since their functionality is defined by the Recommended Standard 232 of the Electronic Industries Alliance (EIA) – an American Standards body.

Serial cables have 9-pin or 25-pin female connectors at each end corresponding to the pins on the ports. A standard serial cable is 'straight through' – that is, pin 1 at one end connects to pin 1 at the other, pin 2 to pin 2, and so on. However, there is a variant which is used for transferring data between two PCs on a direct back-to-back connection where some of the lines are crossed over so that the send pin at one end corresponds with the receive pin at the other. These crossover cables are known as *null modem cables* and can be difficult to distinguish from standard ones.

The standard serial ports and (to a lesser extent) parallel ports are rapidly being superseded by the newer high-speed general purpose ports: USB and FireWire/IEEE 1394.

USB

As personal computing developed, particularly in terms of multimedia devices, the limitations of the older serial ports became all too apparent. In terms of speed and usability, the traditional port did not meet users' needs for fast hassle-free connection of devices such as cameras, external disk drives, etc.

The Universal Serial Bus (USB) was introduced in order to meet the demand for a high-speed port which would allow for the connection of different peripheral devices. The current standard is USB 2. USB is a continually developing technology under the control of the trade association. Details are available from their website at **www.usb.org**.

USB 2 supports three speeds of operation: 1.5Mbps for slow devices such as mice and keyboards, 12Mbps for fast devices (the original speed of USB 1) and 480Mbps which is known as Hi-speed. Most modern systems support the Hi-speed USB 2, but if you have the older USB port, newer devices can still be attached though they will only operate at the lower (USB 1) speed.

One of the major advantages of USB is that it allows 'hot swapping' of components. In order to connect a USB device you simply plug it in to any USB port and the system will sense the change in voltage on the interface, query the device, assign it an identity and load any necessary drivers.

Installing a new USB device needs to be approached with care. Read the installation instructions carefully, preferably twice. In general, most USB devices require you to install drivers before connecting the device. Some may then require a second level of driver installation after connecting. This is not as complicated as it may sound: it's just a matter of doing things in the right order. Chapter 15 covers connecting a USB broadband modem.

There are two standard USB connectors, Type A and Type B. The Type A connector is flat and rectangular in section and the Type B is almost square. The Type A connector is usually at the PC end of the connection with the (smaller) Type B at the device end. There are also 'mini' connectors which are used mainly with small devices such as cameras.

Using one or more USB hubs means that you can connect more devices than you have physical ports on the PC. Typically, you connect a Type A connector at the PC end and a hub at the device end. The hub provides additional Type A ports which can be used to connect other devices (including hubs). In theory, USB can support up to 127 devices simultaneously.

Unlike the older port types, USB is often implemented as a front-of-case port. This makes it easier for the user to take advantage of its hot swapping capabilities.

Low-power devices, such as mice or keyboards, can draw power directly from the host PC (up to 0.5 amps of power per port) but this is obviously unsuitable for power hungry devices such as printers. These need their own external power supply.

When buying a new USB device be sure to check its power requirements and intended speed of operation. If you have to attach a high-speed device to a legacy (USB 1) port it will usually work, but only at a fraction of the USB 2 speed. If you are stuck with USB 1 ports (unlikely on a modern machine) you can add USB 2 ports through a PCI expansion card.

FireWire/IEEE 1394

The Institute of Electrical and Electronic Engineers (IEEE) standard IEEE 1394 defines a standard for a high-speed serial connection which is the main rival to USB. The name FireWire is often applied to all devices conforming to this standard but it is in fact a brand name of Apple Computing Inc. Other brand names which conform to the IEEE 1394 standard include: i.Link (Sony) and Lynx (Texas Instruments). The IEEE 1394 specification is sometimes known as 'Serial SCSI'. Like USB, IEEE 1394 is a continually developing standard. The Trade Association website is **www.1394ta.org** and this is the best source up-to-date information.

The IEEE 1394 connector is bigger than USB with two bevelled edges at the top of the connector so that it can only be connected the right way round. The standard connector has six pins, two of which are for power. There is also a four-pin variant for devices which have their own power supply. This can cause problems when connecting multiple devices in a chain. If you connect a six-pin device 'downstream' of a four-pin device it cannot receive power because there is a break in the power connection to the PC. The answer to this problem is to connect the devices in a different order or to use an external power supply.

Whilst they are different technologies, USB and IEEE 1394 are rivals in the market for high-speed, hot-swappable, easy-to-use connections. At the time of writing the main differences between them is that IEEE 1394 is faster (and usually more expensive) and it supports *isochronous* data transfers (i.e. real time transfers) which make it particularly suitable for transferring audio and video data at the same time. For this reason, it is often the technology of choice for data transfers from – or between – movie cameras. Where the cameras – or other devices – support it, IEEE 1394 can manage transfers of data between devices without being attached to a host PC.

All modern Windows versions support IEEE 1394, just as they do USB. If your PC doesn't have IEEE 1394 ports they can be added through a PCI expansion card. There are even cards which provide a mixture of IEEE 1394 and USB ports.

10.4 Device drivers

A device driver is a piece of software that enables a hardware component to communicate with the rest of the PC. Drivers may be supplied with the Windows Operating System, on a disk – usually a CD – included in the manufacturer's packaging of the device, or downloaded from the manufacturer's website.

Installing device drivers

Many common devices, such as the more popular network cards (internal devices) or printers (external or peripheral) devices are supported by Windows 'out of the box'. That is to say, when

Windows 'discovers' a new device it will look for a suitable driver and if there is one, will install it with the minimum of user intervention.

The drivers which are supplied with Windows are probably adequate for the job. They may even be the best drivers for the job, but there is no guarantee of this. Technology moves quickly and the drivers that were shipped with Windows may have been superseded by newer ones.

Where a device has manufacturer's drivers – usually supplied on a CD and packaged with the retail product – these may offer enhanced capabilities or better performance that the ones supplied with Windows. The older your Windows version, the more likely this is to be the case.

A third possibility, is that the manufacturer has updated the drivers for the device since it was assembled and packed and made available for retail sales (possibly several months before) and that the latest and best drivers can be downloaded from their website.

Whatever the source of your device drivers, check the product and its documentation before using them as there are different approaches to installing them on your system.

The most straightforward case is the device which plugs and plays and then prompts for drivers. Providing the drivers are bundled with the operating system or you have them on CD all you need to do is to follow the instructions on the screen. You may well have to reboot the system in order to complete the process, but it is essentially a straightforward one.

Some devices, however – particularly USB devices – require you to install drivers *before* adding or attaching the hardware. If you don't do this you will probably end up with a device that doesn't work – or doesn't work properly. If this happens, cut your losses, uninstall the drivers (use Add/Remove Programs from the Control Panel to do this – you will need Administrator rights) and start again. As someone said: '*When all else fails, try reading the instructions!*'

Occasionally, you may come across a device which has a two-stage process for driver installation: install drivers, attach device, install further drivers – usually with a reboot somewhere in the sequence of events.

Elsewhere in the book, there are worked examples of installing device drivers which illustrate these points:

* Adding a wireless network interface card – Chapter 17

* Installing a printer and setting up a share – Chapter 11

* Installing a USB broadband modem – Chapter 15.

Signed drivers

When installing device drivers you may receive a warning from Windows that the driver is 'unsigned' – this is usually nothing to worry about.

Microsoft have a scheme whereby manufacturers can submit a driver for testing and, providing it meets the necessary criteria it may be approved by Microsoft as being compatible with their Windows operating system – this is a 'signed' driver.

For various reasons, manufacturers do not necessarily follow these procedures for the 'signing' of their products and there are even installation instructions supplied with a device which tell you to ignore the warning and proceed anyway.

Summary

This chapter has examined the common ports that you can expect to find on a modern PC. You should be able to distinguish these ports by sight as well as the cables and connectors that go with them. In general, things only fit one way into the port of the correct size and type (though watch out for the two types of cable which can be fitted to the older style serial port).

We have looked at device drivers and how to install them and noted that reading the manual or the installation instructions before starting work can save a lot of time and frustration.

11

printers

In this chapter you will learn:

- about common printer types
- how to connect a printer and install drivers
- how to share a printer on a network
- what to do if your printer doesn't work

11.1 Printers and PCs

Printers are peripheral devices which attach to one of the standard ports on the PC, so it may be useful to refer back to Chapter 10, *Peripheral devices* as background information for this topic.

Printers usually attach to the parallel port on the PC (which is why it is frequently referred to as 'the printer port') or increasingly nowadays to one of the USB ports. Very occasionally you may encounter a 'serial printer' which attaches to the older style 9-pin or 25-pin serial port.

Of all the devices which you may want to attach to your PC, a printer is probably the most complex and most likely to have non-standard features. Whereas the PC is based on some well-known industry standards, printers are considerably more diverse in what they do and how they do it. For example, most printers have some sort of test routines built into them. You may, for instance, be able to print a test page from a printer which isn't connected to a PC by holding down a particular combination of function keys on the printer as it powers up. However, the precise nature of the test and the key combination needed to access it will vary from printer to printer. The standard advice to read the manual first is especially important when working with a printer.

11.2 Common printer types

The main printer types in use today are:

- Dot matrix (increasingly uncommon)
- Ink jet (and bubble jet)
- Laser
- Multi-function (usually based on an ink jet or laser jet).

There are other printer types for specialized work – photographic, dye sublimation, thermal, wax jet, and so on. These are not normally used by home or even small office users, so we will concentrate on the main types only.

Dot matrix

The dot matrix printer type is not often used these days except where verifiable multiple copies (such as an invoice or sales receipt) are required.

The principle of the dot matrix printer is simple. Paper is drawn through the printer around a cylinder (the platen) in much the same way as it was in the old style manual typewriter. Letters and images are made up of ink dots and these are made by striking through a typewriter style ribbon onto the paper. The printer has an array of pins – or printwires – and it traverses the length of a print line, forming the outline shapes of letters by striking through the ribbon. Common numbers of printwires on a print head are 9, 18, or 24. The greater the number of printwires the better the quality of the output. Using 24 pins or multiple passes over the same line can deliver *Near Letter Quality* (NLQ) output.

Dot matrix printers are durable devices and need little in the way of maintenance. The platen and the print head can be cleaned with denatured alcohol, and gears and pulleys lightly lubricated. Don't allow lubricant near the print head as this will cause the print output to smear. Perhaps the most important thing is to replace the ribbon in a timely fashion. Because the output from an inked ribbon fades gradually through time it is easy not to notice how faded the output has become – until you replace it!

Ink jet/bubble jet

Ink jet and bubble jet printers (known collectively as ink dispersion printers) are very popular with home and micro-business users. They are slightly more expensive to run than laser printers in terms of consumables – ink/toner – but they are reasonably priced and can produce full colour output which varies in quality between draft and photographic. Using specialized papers can further increase the quality of the finished printed output.

Ink jets form an image by squirting very small dots of ink on to the paper. The print quality is measured by the number of these dots per inch and may range from 150 dots per inch (DPI) to 1400 (and higher).

Ink jet printer speeds are rated in pages per minute (rather than characters per second) because the ink jet doesn't form each character separately, it prints a line across the page which contains only a portion of the image whether character or graphic. Most inkjets print bi-directionally and produce 2–9 pages per minute (PPM).

The paper feed mechanism on ink jets may be single sheet manual feed but is usually a cut-sheet feeder. The paper is fed past the print head by a series of rollers that hold it in place. It is advanced one print line at a time. The finished page is stacked face up.

There are various arrangements for supplying ink. Usually there is a reservoir of black ink and a combined red/blue/yellow reservoir, though increasingly these days the coloured inks each have a separate reservoir.

Some printers have the print head built into the reservoir so that the electronics are replaced every time the ink is renewed; other printers have the print head built in so that only the ink and its container are replaced. There is a price/reliability trade-off here and this may be one of the considerations when evaluating a potential printer.

Common problems with ink jet printers

The main problem encountered with ink jet and bubble jet printers is the tendency for the ink to dry and clog the nozzles. To counter this all ink jet printers move the print head to a special position known variously as the park, cleaning or maintenance area.

Most ink jet and bubble printers have some sort of head cleaning or diagnostic mode built into them which is accessed by holding down some combination of keys. This is probably specific to the make or model of printer so you should consult the manual for your printer. There is also software support for cleaning and aligning print heads as a supplement to the printer drivers on the manufacturer's disk for many printer models. If you can't find such a utility on your driver disk it may be worth visiting the printer manufacturer's website to see if such a utility (possibly as part of an updated driver package) may be available.

Laser printers

The laser printer is pretty much the standard choice for business users because of its lower running costs and quality of print finish. A print from an ink jet, for example, will 'run' if it becomes wet, whereas the laser process produces a very stable finish.

In recent years, laser printers have become more reasonably priced – a black-only laser desktop printer can be bought for well under £100 – so laser printers are now an option for some home users.

The laser printing process is similar to the working of a photocopier. It uses a fine dust of toner to create the required image on paper and this is fused on to the finished print by passing it through a heated roller known as a 'fuser'. This accounts for the slightly 'cooked' feel of a printout when it emerges from the printer.

The heat involved in the laser printing process also means that you need to be careful when printing onto transparencies for overhead projectors. Make sure that you are using transparencies that are intended for use in laser printers. If you use anything else – transparencies which are intended for an ink jet or hand writing – they will melt as they pass through the printer and it will be severely damaged – probably to the point of being a complete write-off.

Maintenance tasks with laser printers

Apart from general cleaning – removal of dust and paper debris, etc. – there is little to go wrong with the mechanism of a laser printer that can be serviced by the user. You will need to replace the toner when it runs out, of course, and on many laser printers this consists of dropping in a complete unit which means that many of the components which are sensitive to everyday wear and tear are replaced as a matter of course.

Many of the more expensive laser printers – such as the Hewlett Packard LaserJet series – can be refurbished from maintenance kits which provide replacements for components which are known to be prone to wear and failure on that particular model.

Common problems with laser printers

Probably the most common cause of poor quality prints from a laser printer is the wrong type of paper or other printing surface. If there are problems with print quality, the first thing to check is the paper. Break open a new packet of standard photocopy paper and try printing on that. If this cures the problem then your printer is okay, but your print surface is not. This can be the result of using the wrong type of surface – too smooth or too rough at the microscopic level – or inappropriate storage conditions for your paper stock.

If inappropriate print surfaces have been ruled out then you may have a hardware problem. Most laser printers have some form of diagnostic self-test mode and this is useful if only to establish whether the problem encountered is in the printer itself or in the PC which is the source of the print job.

If you have problems, try the following:

- Replace the toner cartridge

- Check cabling

- Replace the data cable

- Turn off any advanced functions.

If none of these work it is probably not a user serviceable problem. For an expensive professional office printer, you may be able to take it to a registered service centre. For the cheaper models the best solution may be replacement.

Multi-function printers/scanners

There has been a massive growth in the popularity of multi-function printers in recent years. These are usually based on ink jet technology, but they offer a range of features over and above simple printing.

Typically, a multi-function printer will also be a scanner, photo-copier and fax machine and may well have a slot where you can insert the memory card from a digital camera and print your photographs directly from it.

Multi-function printers vary considerably in their details between makes and models so it is especially important to consult any documentation or manuals provided with the product that are specific to it.

Whatever the details of your particular make and model, there are some general maintenance guidelines. In addition to checking the quality and condition of the paper, cable connections, ink levels, and running head cleaning routines, you may need to clean the inside of the printer.

- Disconnect the printer form the mains supply

- Remove any covers or access panels

- Remove any dust, dirt or debris from the interior

- Clean internal parts with a dry cotton swab or lint-free cloth

- Remove any stubborn deposits by dipping the swab or cloth in a *very small* amount of water or denatured alcohol

- Make sure that everything is clean and dry before replacing covers, powering up and testing.

After doing these maintenance tasks you may have to recalibrate the printer/scanner. You will need to follow the detailed instructions in the manufacturer's manual to do this.

11.3 Printer connection methods

Connecting to the parallel port

The commonest way of connecting a printer to a PC is through the parallel port on the back of the machine. A standard parallel printer cable has a 25-pin male end which attaches to the port on the back of the PC and a Centronics connector which attaches to the printer. (These are very distinctive in appearance and can only fit one way.) Connect the printer to the PC with the printer cable and turn it on. Unless it is something very unusual, Windows will detect it and it will plug and play. You may have to provide drivers as part of the installation process. For a guide to installation see section 11.4, *Installing a printer*.

Connecting to a USB port

Connecting a printer to a USB port is similar to using the parallel port. The USB cable will have a Type 'A' end – flat and rectangular in section and a smaller Type 'B' connector which goes at the printer end. Even if you have front USB ports, it is probably as well to connect the printer to one of the ports at the back of the machine and save your front ports for equipment such as cameras or flash memory sticks where you may want to use the hot swap capabilities of USB.

Connect the Type 'B' connector to the printer and power it up. **Do not** connect to the PC until you have read the installation instructions that came with the printer. Most USB printers require you to install drivers before connecting to the PC and if you don't do this you will probably end up with a printer that is 'installed' but which won't actually work.

With the necessary drivers installed, plug the Type 'A' connector to the port on the PC and turn the printer on. Follow the instructions on screen to complete the installation process – see also the next section.

11.4 Installing a printer

This section walks through installing an Epson Photo 890 printer on a parallel port on a PC running Windows XP Home Edition. There may be some minor differences between printer makes and types and different Windows versions but it should serve as a generic guide to the process.

Before you start, make sure that you have the documentation and the driver disk that came with the printer. As this particular printer has both a parallel interface and a USB interface, decide which of them you are going to use and make sure that you have the appropriate cable.

Unpack the printer and read the setup instructions – twice!

1 Put the CD with the drivers in the CD drive. If it doesn't auto-run, navigate to it through the My Computer icon. You will see something like the content of Figure 11.01.

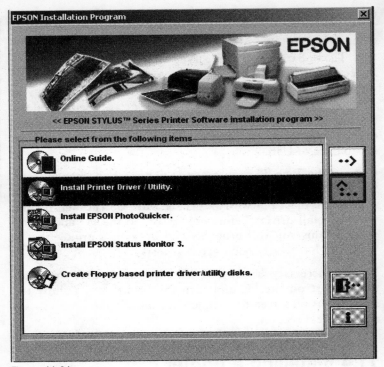

Figure 11.01

2 Choose the **Install Printer Driver/Utility** option and select the right-facing arrow to continue.

3 Choose the printer model (in this case there is only one).

The system will confirm that the installation is under way.

4 The installation program will want to know whether you are going to use the parallel port or the USB port to connect your printer. In this example we are using the parallel port, so follow the instructions on screen in order to **Stop Searching**.

5 At this point, if you were using the USB interface, you would connect the printer and turn it on. The installer would then detect the printer and do the necessary software installation. In this example, we are using the parallel port so we proceed to step 6 below.

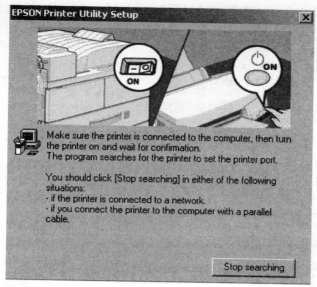

Make sure the printer is connected to the computer, then turn the printer on and wait for confirmation.
The program searches for the printer to set the printer port.

You should click [Stop searching] in either of the following situations:
- if the printer is connected to a network.
- if you connect the printer to the computer with a parallel cable.

Stop searching

Figure 11.02

6 The installer installs supplementary utilities so that you can monitor ink levels and run cleaning routines once your printer is installed.

7 Connect the printer to the parallel port and turn it on as shown in Figure 11.03.

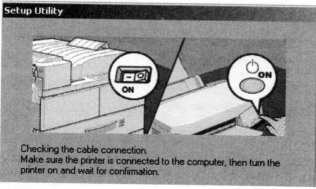

Checking the cable connection.
Make sure the printer is connected to the computer, then turn the printer on and wait for confirmation.

Figure 11.03

8 The system confirms that the printer has been installed to the Port LPT1 – the parallel port – which is what we wanted.

9 Finally, open the Printers and Faxes applet in the Control Panel to confirm that the new printer is installed and is the new default printer.

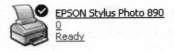

Figure 11.04

10 At this point you may want to print a test page to satisfy yourself that your new printer is installed and working. Right-click on the printer's icon and select **Properties** from the context menu. This will open at the **General** tab. Click **Print Test Page** as shown in Figure 11.05.

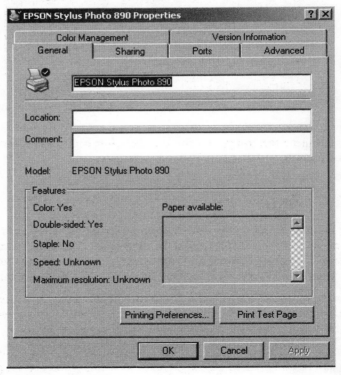

Figure 11.05

11.5 Sharing a printer on a network

In order to make your newly installed printer available on your network you need to create a *Share*.

1 Run the **Printers and Faxes** applet in the Control Panel.

2 Right-click on the printer Icon and select **Sharing....**

3 Check the **Share this printer** radio button and give the printer a meaningful name.

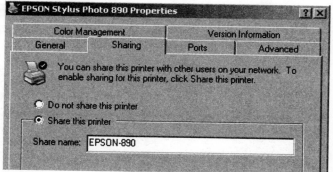

Figure 11.06

The share name of the printer – in this case EPSON-890 – is what will be seen on your network. Installing a network printer is considered in Chapter 17, *Home networking*.

11.6 Obtaining drivers and manuals

If you have bought your printer from a retailer (local or online) you may want to obtain manuals or drivers for it from the manufacturer's website. You may simply want to be sure that you have the very latest drivers for your printer and operating system.

Obviously, the exact procedures will vary between manufacturers and possibly models. The following worked example shows how to do this for the Epson 890 used in the previous example.

1 The first thing to do, of course, is to check the exact name and model number of the printer. With this information, go to the manufacturer's website. In this example it is

www.epson.com. You will be prompted for your region and country. Having selected these, you will be transferred to another page within the site.

2 Within this page you will see a section entitled **Drivers & Support**. Choose the product type and model from the drop-down lists and click **Go**.

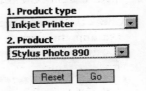

Drivers & Support

Please choose from the drop-down menus to get support for your Epson product:

1. Product type

Inkjet Printer

2. Product

Stylus Photo 890

Reset Go

Figure 11.07

3 This takes you to the page for your printer model. The next step is to choose first your operating system (XP), then choose **Setup Guides and Manuals** or **Driver and software downloads**. These will both take you to the page shown here.

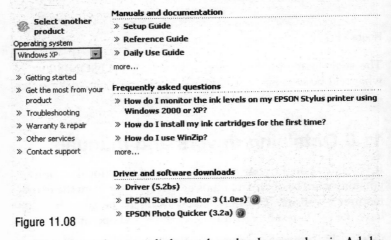

Figure 11.08

4 From here there are links to download manuals – in Adobe PDF format – as well as binary drivers for your operating system and printer. If you download the manuals and don't already have a copy of the Adobe Acrobat Reader program installed on your system you can download a copy of this program free from **www.adobe.com**.

5   For purposes of this example, we will just download the main XP driver software for XP. In order to do this, click on the link **Driver** under the **Driver and software downloads** heading. Depending on the speed of your Internet connection this may take 13 or so minutes on a standard dialup connection or a minute and a half over 512 Mbps broadband – faster, if your Internet connection is faster than this.

6   The driver package is supplied in the form of a self-extracting Zip file. You will need to unzip this file to a suitable location. The best way of doing this is to create one. Since this is a temporary measure you can do this on the Desktop.

7   For this example I created a new folder on the XP Desktop and called it *Epson-890-Drivers*.

8   Click on the downloaded self-extracting Zip file and click the **OK** button on the welcome screen. This takes you to the dialog box shown in Figure 11.09. Select **Browse** and navigate to the folder which you created earlier.

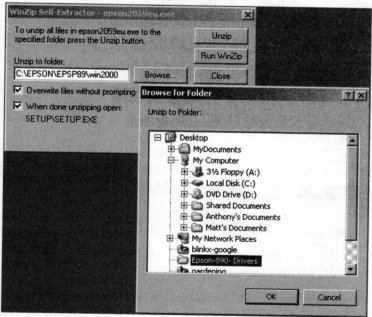

Figure 11.09

9 Select **OK**, then click **Unzip**. The unzip utility will take a few seconds to complete. When it has done so close it and click on the *Epson-890-Drivers* folder which you created earlier. You will see the unzipped files – 47 of them in this case – and you can run the installer program from here.

Having downloaded your drivers, you may want to download any other available software utilities and manual from the manufacturer's site and burn them all to CD for future use. If you do this, it would be sensible to create a separate folder for each with a meaningful name such as *Drivers*, *Manuals*, etc. Once saved to CD you may safely delete the temporary folder which you created on the Desktop.

11.7 What to do if your printer doesn't work

Most printing problems are printer problems. As with most things, the first thing to do is to check the obvious: is the printer turned on and connected to the PC? Does it have paper in the feed tray? Are there any lights flashing that might indicate that one or more of the ink cartridges are empty? If you have more than one printer on the system make sure you are printing to the correct one!

If you have sent a print job to the printer, you should see a printer icon in the Notification Area at the bottom right end of the Taskbar (this is sometimes referred to by the older name of the System Tray). Clicking on this icon will bring up the Print Queue for your printer as shown in Figure 11.10.

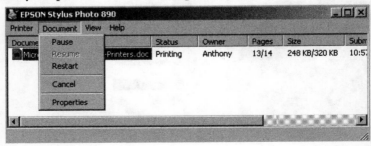

Figure 11.10

From here you can obtain information about the print job, pause it, restart it, or cancel it altogether. Sometimes, cancelling the print job altogether, then starting afresh by printing from the application will be sufficient to fix the problem.

Having checked the obvious again you can uninstall and reinstall the printer drivers. If this doesn't work, you probably have hardware problems that are beyond the scope of what a home user can do. If your printer is something big, or expensive, or is still under warranty it may be worth calling in outside help. On the other hand, this may be a good time to buy something new!

Summary

This chapter has looked at printer types and connections, and how to care for, clean and maintain you printer. We have seen a worked example of the process of connecting a particular make and model of printer to a PC, installing software drivers for it and how to make it available as a network share on your home network. There will, of course, be some variations on this according to your particular make and model of printer.

A further worked example illustrates the process of downloading drivers and manuals for a popular make and model of printer – again, this is an outline example which may differ in some details from your particular make and model of printer.

Finally, we have considered the most common causes of a failure to print and possible solutions.

12 components and programs

In this chapter you will learn:

- how to add, change or remove programs
- how to add/remove Windows components
- about program access and defaults

12.1 Add/remove components and applications

To get the best out of your system you need to be able to add and remove both Windows components (programs and utilities that are supplied with Windows, e.g. Outlook Express or Windows Mail) and applications such as the Office suite.

The examples here are taken from Windows XP Professional. XP Home works almost identically. The same functionality is available in Vista, though you may have to explore the Programs and Default Programs options in the Control Panel to find the details. There are notes in the text to help you do this.

12.2 Making changes to your system

In order to make any system-level changes in any modern Windows version you need Administrator privileges. If you are running one of the Home editions of Windows you may have enough rights to do the things outlined in this chapter using your everyday user account. However, if you get a message telling you that you don't have the necessary permissions, you will need to log in using the Administrator account before making modifications.

As with all but the most trivial of system alterations it is prudent to set a System Restore point before starting work. See Chapter 2, *System tools* if you can't remember how to do this.

To carry out the tasks described in this chapter you need to navigate to the Control Panel with Administrator privileges. If the Control Panel is in Category View, click on the Switch to Classic View option – at the top left of the window.

In Classic View, Add/Remove Programs is usually in the third or fourth place in the list – the highlighted option in Figure 12.01.

Accessibility Options   Add Hardware   Add or Remove Programs   Administrative Tools   Belkin Wireless Utility

Figure 12.01

The Add/Remove Programs panel lists four options and by default it starts up with the *Change or Remove Programs* option open. The four choices are listed down the left side of the panel and the contents in the pane to the right. By default, the program listing is in alphabetical order, though this can be changed through the drop-down list at the top right of the panel.

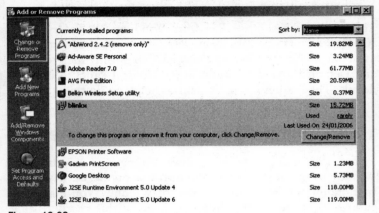

Figure 12.02

As you can see from Figure 12.02 there are four top-level options in the left pane, each of which corresponds to a detailed list of programs or components on the right. These are:

* Change or Remove Programs
* Add New Programs
* Add/Remove Windows Components
* Set Program Access and Defaults.

12.3 Change or Remove Programs

(Control Panel > Programs > Installed Programs in Vista)

If you wanted to label any of the options as the core workhorse of the Add/Remove Programs utility, then this would be it. Every installed application on your system is listed here along with information about its size, frequency of use, and date of last use. There is also a button to remove the program in question.

The highlighted program in Figure 12.03 is an application called Blinkx and the system shows that it is seldom used.

To remove it:

1   Click **Change/Remove**. This will start the Uninstall wizard for that program. Uninstall programs may vary somewhat in their details, but the *Blinkx* example is fairly typical.

2   The Uninstall wizard presents a window that prompts you to select either an automatic or a custom uninstall. Don't bother with custom unless you are interested in the details of the process; just select automatic (the default) and click **Next**.

3   You will be presented with a screen which asks you whether or not you wish to proceed with the uninstall process. This is your last opportunity to say 'no'. If you wish to continue with the uninstall, click **Finish**. The uninstaller shuts down running processes associated with Blinkx.

4   The uninstaller then runs and reports its progress as shown in Figure 12.03.

5   At the end of the uninstall process you may be prompted to reboot your computer in order to complete the process.

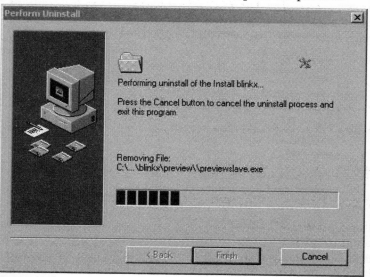

Figure 12.03

Most uninstallers will work more or less as described in this example, though not all are particularly well written. The step of shutting down running processes may not be built in and you may receive an error message along the lines of 'This program is currently in use by another process'. If this happens you may have to exit the uninstaller and turn off the offending process. This is frequently caused by Quick Launch icons in the System Tray/Notification Area. Usually these can be turned off by right-clicking on the icon in the tray and selecting **Exit** or **Quit**.

If you need to, you can access the Task Manager by holding down [Ctrl]+[Alt]+[Del]. This will show you a list of running programs and processes and give you the opportunity to kill them off – highlight the relevant entry in the list and click **End Process**. If you do this, you receive a warning that ending a process

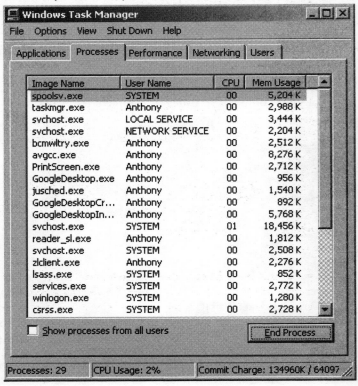

Figure 12.04

may destabilize the system. This may be the case, especially if you have chosen the wrong process! However, any damage done will only affect the current session and can be reversed by rebooting your PC.

Finally, no matter how well written the uninstaller may be, there will probably be some redundant files somewhere that haven't been removed. For example, the Blinkx uninstaller that we have looked at leaves a folder called *Blinkx* in *C:\Program Files*. To remove the contents of this folder, right-click on it and choose **Delete** from the context menu. If you don't want to do this, leave it in place – it will take up some disk space but will otherwise do no harm.

12.4 Add New Programs

The Add New Programs utility contains two options: Add programs from Microsoft and Add a program from CD-ROM or floppy disk, as shown in Figure 12.05.

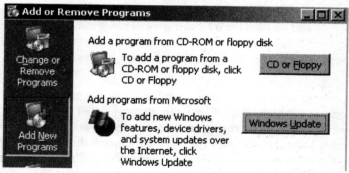

Figure 12.05

1   **Add programs from Microsoft** – as the button suggests – is a shortcut to the Windows Update site. To visit this (assuming that you are online), click the button. Once you have connected to the site your system will be remotely examined and you will be asked what you want to do next. In this example, the Windows Update software is out of date and the site suggests downloading the latest version.

(i) Get the latest
Windows Update software.

We've made improvements to our
website. To download the new version
of the software and begin using
Windows Update, please click Install
Now.

Install Now

Figure 12.06

2   If you wish to proceed, click **Install Now**. Once the update is in place you will be presented with various options according to the remote analysis of your system. You may choose to install whatever options you want and you can set the system to automate the update process in future.

The **Add a program from CD-ROM or floppy disk** option just prompts you to place the installation CD or floppy disk in the drive and click **Next**. The system then searches the drives for installation programs. There is no difference between putting in the disk and waiting for it to autoplay or navigating to it through Windows Explorer. Another common way of installing software is from an installer downloaded from the Internet.

Regardless of whether you install from a disk or a downloaded file the process is essentially similar. Navigate to the installer program – which is often (but not always) called SETUP.EXE – click on its icon to run it, and follow the instructions on the screen. Most installation programs will unpack themselves, copy files to predetermined locations on your hard disk, update the Registry and create Desktop or Taskbar icons to launch the new program. For some, you may have to enter a product key – if it is commercial software – and there may be an online registration process. You will almost certainly have to reboot your PC at some point before the new software can be used. Nearly all installation software requires Administrator privileges – so log in using the Administrator user account if necessary.

The following worked example shows the installation of the free Open Office suite on a Windows XP Home PC. It is fairly typical of the installation process for any piece of software.

Installing Open Office – a worked example

Open Office is a free office suite, similar in its scope to Microsoft Office. It doesn't have all of the advanced features of Microsoft Office, but it has all that most users need: a word processor, a spreadsheet and so forth. Figure 12.07 shows the components of the current version of Open Office as displayed on their website, **www.openoffice.org**. Apart from being useful, it is free!

Figure 12.07

Open Office is available with support for many languages and for operating systems other than Windows, such as Macintosh, Solaris and Linux. You can download relevant documentation such as a Setup Guide, User Guide and Release Notes from the Open Office site.

You can download the latest version of Open Office from their site, or you may find it distributed on (say) a magazine cover disk. In this example, we will install it from a CD-ROM through the Add a program from CD-ROM or floppy disk option.

1   Open the Control Panel and navigate to the required **Add a program...** option and click the **CD or Floppy** button.

2   You will be prompted to put the CD with the installation program into the CD drive. Do this, then click **Next**. Windows searches the floppy then the CD drives. If there is an installer on the CD it will show the filename in a dialog box.

3   If the file is correct, just click **Finish** to run the installer. If, for any reason, it is not the correct one, clicking **Browse** will allow you to look at all the files on the CD.

♦   In this example, we have started the installer through the Add/Remove applet. We could just as well have clicked on the installer file on the CD through My Computer, or on the downloaded file on the hard disk or the Desktop. Regardless of how or from where we start the installer, the process will be the same.

4 The first screen that the Open Office installer shows is the Welcome screen. Click on **Next** to continue or **Cancel** to stop.

5 You will be prompted to make the installation folder on your hard disk. Accept what the installer suggests by clicking on **Unpack**. The installer now decompresses the files it needs. This may take a couple of minutes or so. When this is done the Installation Wizard will run. It will examine your system – again this may take a minute or so – then you will be presented with a screen like the one shown in Figure 12.08.

Figure 12.08

6 Click on **Next**, then accept the terms of the licence agreement and click **Next** again. This will take you to a screen where you can personalize the software and make it available for all users of the system, as in Figure 12.09.

7 Click **Next** again to reach a screen where you can choose a Complete install (all the components) or a Custom install where you choose which features you want. In this example, we will choose the default Complete install by clicking on **Next**. You will then be asked whether you want to use Open Office to open Word, Excel and PowerPoint files instead of the Microsoft programs which were used to create them.

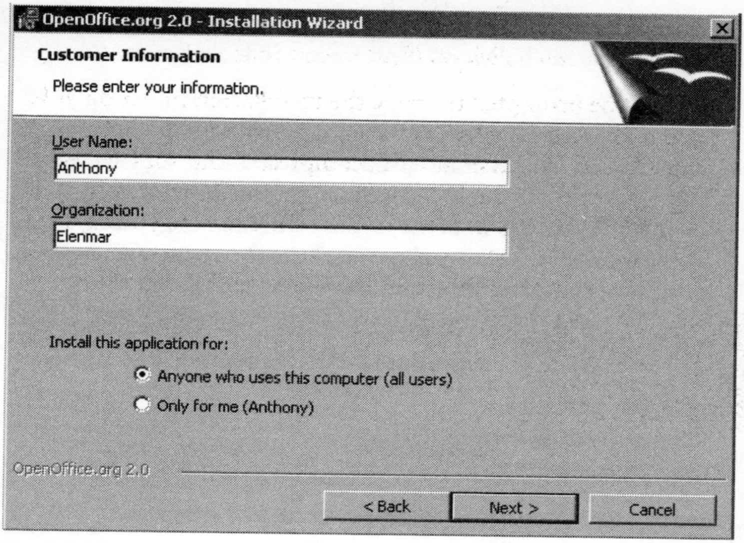

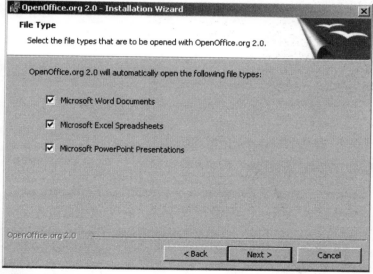

Figure 12.09

Figure 12.10

8 If you tick the boxes as shown in Figure 12.10, clicking on, say, a Word document will cause it to be opened using the

Open Office Writer program. You can also edit and save documents in the Word .doc format which can be read by people who have the paid-for Microsoft program instead of the free Open Office one.

9 Click **Next**. You will be given a last chance to go back and change your choices or to cancel the installation. Click on **Install** to start the final stage. Just sit back and watch – this will probably take several minutes. At the end of this process click **Finish** to exit from the installer.

10 If you open the **Start** menu and navigate to **All Programs** you can see the newly installed **Open Office** components as shown in Figure 12.11.

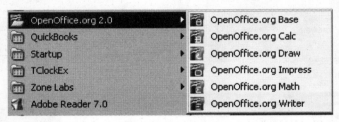

Figure 12.11

When you start one of the *Open Office* components – such as the *Writer* – for the first time, you can customize it further in terms of appearance, etc.

12.5 Add/Remove Windows Components

(Control Panel > Programs > Windows Features in Vista)

Windows components are not, technically, part of the operating system, but applications which are bundled with it. According to your needs as a user, you can add or remove components such as games or fax services. To access the Add/Remove Windows Components utility, navigate to it through the Control Panel and click on the appropriate icon. You will see the options shown in Figure 12.12.

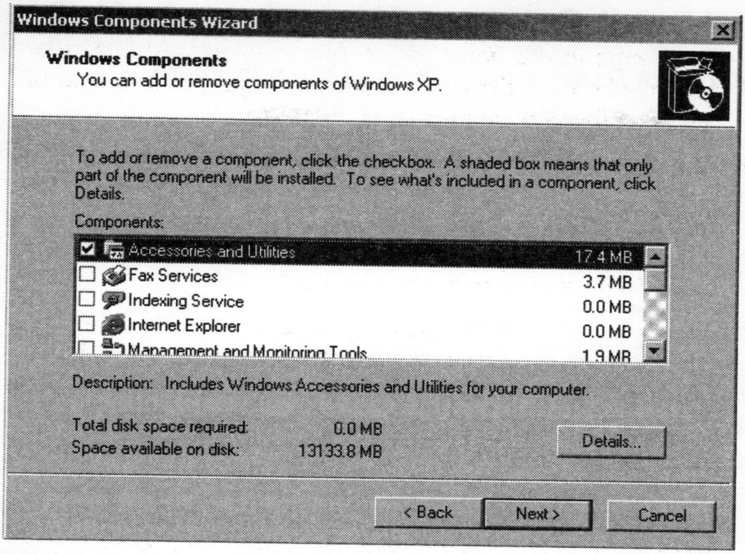

Figure 12.12

The boxes to the left of the figure are white where none of that group of components are installed, white with a tick where all elements of that group are installed, and grey with a tick where some elements are installed. Where there are sub-options, you can see these by highlighting the entry and clicking **Details**.

Windows components are added or removed by ticking (or unticking) the box next to a component and clicking on **Next**. In the example shown in Figure 12.12, the Internet Explorer browser is not installed. To install it:

1 Click on the empty checkbox (to tick it), then click **Next**. The system will display a progress bar as it updates the required components.

2 When it finishes, the Wizard displays a notice to this effect. Click **Finish** and the job is complete. Internet Explorer will now be available for use and will show up as installed if you re-examine the Windows Components list.

Depending on the initial configuration of your system there may also be a Quick Launch icon added to the left of the Taskbar and/or a Desktop icon.

12.6 Set Program Access and Defaults

(Control Panel > Default Programs in Vista)

To use this option, navigate to the Control Panel and click the appropriate icon. You will see a list like the one in Figure 12.13.

A program configuration specifies default programs for certain activities, such as Web browsing or sending e-mail, and which programs are accessible from the Start menu, desktop, and other locations.

Choose a configuration:

○ Microsoft Windows	✹
○ Non-Microsoft	✹
◉ Custom	✹

Figure 12.13

The list has three elements: one for Windows Programs, one for non-Microsoft programs and a third labelled Custom. Click the chevron to the right of the element to see a drop-down list. The first two will give you information about the current configuration; the Custom list allows you to change things. Figure 12.14 shows the Custom list.

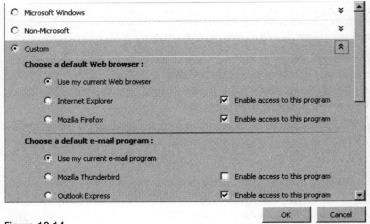

Figure 12.14

In the example shown in the figure, the user has downloaded and installed the Firefox Web browser. If you wish to do this, you can visit **www.mozilla.com** where you can download the

Firefox browser free. (There's also an excellent free email program called Thunderbird available from the same site. Many people use this as an alternative to Outlook Express/Windows Mail which is bundled with Windows.)

Having installed Firefox you may wish to reconfigure the system so that it becomes the default browser instead of Internet Explorer and to remove (or at least make inaccessible) the Internet Explorer browser. In order to do this, check the radio button to the left of the Firefox entry in the list and uncheck the box to the right of the Internet Explorer entry as shown in Figure 12.15.

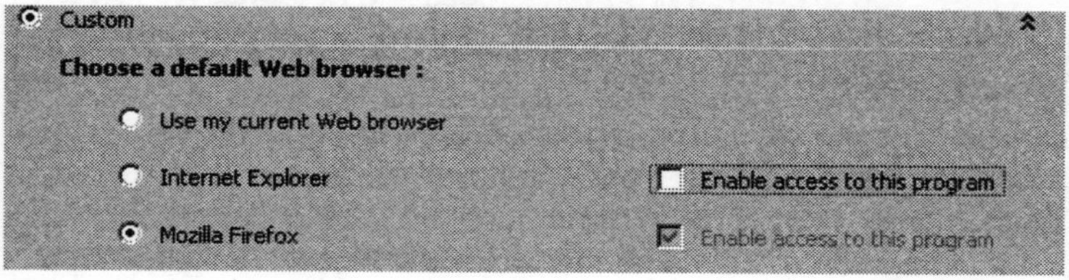

Figure 12.15

When you have done this click **OK**. The system will make the requested changes, removing access to Internet Explorer and setting Firefox as the default browser.

Figure 12.16

The system offers the possibility of cancelling the changes if you wish. If you let it run to the end, Internet Explorer will have been removed from both the Desktop and the Quick Launch toolbar. Even a search on the term IEXPLORE will yield a negative result.

Obviously, you can install and configure any application along these lines. Another freebie worth mentioning is the Opera web browser which you can download and install as an alternative to IE or Firefox.

Summary

In this chapter we have looked at the Windows utilities which you can use to add or remove application programs and Windows components. We have examined the utility which allows you to change program access and defaults. We have walked through some examples of these tasks using freely available (and free) software.

With the knowledge you have gained from this chapter you should be able to carry out these tasks and if you don't like them you can always reverse them. The best way to learn anything on a PC is to have a go and if it goes really wrong all modern Windows versions have the System Restore utility to roll the system back to a previous known good state.

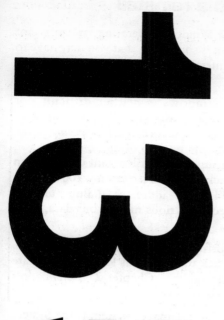

13

installing/ reinstalling Windows

In this chapter you will learn:

- how to avoid a reinstall
- how to prepare for a reinstall
- how to perform an OEM install
- how to perform a conventional install

13.1 How to avoid a reinstall

Installing or reinstalling the Windows operating system is not an everyday task. However, it is something that you may have to do after a very severe virus infection, for example, or a hard disk failure.

Installing or reinstalling Windows is neither difficult nor complicated. However, it is time-consuming and will destroy *all* the contents of your hard disk so before doing *anything* make sure that you have an up-to-date backup of all your data. You should also try restoring a couple of test files from your backup just to make sure that the backup system is working 100%. Even key settings like your email server addresses, dialup numbers and so forth can be replaced by various means, but data, once gone, is gone for good.

If your system has become corrupt because of some recent change, you can, of course, roll it back to a previous known good state by using the System Restore utility – Chapter 2, *System tools* takes you through the process of doing this.

Another quick and easy fix for a damaged system is the System File Check utility. This has been available since the days of Windows 98. To use this utility, go to a 'Run' box or a command prompt and type in the command SFC /SCANNOW, followed by a carriage return. You will need Administrator rights to do this. You will see a screen like the one in Figure 13.01.

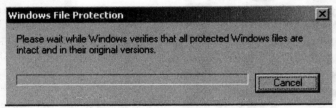

Figure 13.01

What happens next depends on the type of installation you have on your PC. If you have an OEM install (see below), the System File Check will begin; if you have a conventional install you will be prompted for the installation disk as shown in Figure 13.02.

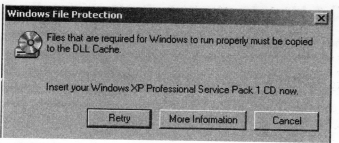

Figure 13.02

Whichever option you have chosen, the system will start a System File Check. As you will see from Figure 13.03, Windows starts the process of verifying that 'all protected Windows files are intact and in their original versions'.

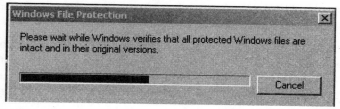

Figure 13.03

At this stage the SFC utility displays a progress bar. This file check is usually a fairly slow process – there are a lot of files to check! There is a Cancel button to end the process if necessary.

If Windows finds that there is a difference between a system file on your hard disk and its original version on the installation CD it will report the fact to you and give you the option to replace the damaged or corrupted file. If there are no problems, the System File Check utility simply exits without any kind of message to you. In this case, no news is good news – all of your protected system files are intact and in their original versions.

After running SFC, reboot the PC – always good practice to reboot after making any changes – and test for stability and proper operation. If your system is now working properly then you won't need to reinstall Windows. If you are still having problems, you may decide to reinstall it. The key to doing this with the minimum of inconvenience to yourself or any other users of the PC is to prepare for the job beforehand.

13.2 How to prepare for a reinstall

The key to a successful reinstall is preparation. The first thing to do is a backup of all your data. Providing you have some sort of backup regime in place, this is easy – just run your backup system and put the backup media somewhere safe. (Remember to test!) If you don't have a backup system in place, now might be a good time to set one up – see Chapter 6, *Backup strategies*. Alternatively, you may like to use the Files and Settings Transfer Wizard (XP) or the Easy Transfer Wizard (Vista) – more on this later.

As a further preparation, check that you have any software drivers for peripheral devices such as printers, scanners, external modems and so forth. If anything is missing or out of date, now is the time to visit manufacturers' websites in order to download what is needed and burn it to CD or other removable storage.

Finally, make sure that you have a record of any setting that you want to save and restore. As a minimum you should be sure to have user names, passwords, access codes, etc. so that you can connect to the Internet and send and receive email. That way, you are not too far from help if you need it. You could use the Files and Settings Transfer Wizard for this but this is putting rather a lot of eggs in the same electronic basket. There are some key settings that are best kept as ink on paper in a safe place.

Data

This is straightforward. Use your existing backup system to make sure that you have a fully up-to-date backup of your data. If you don't have a system for doing this, save the essential files to a removable medium such as CD/DVD, a pen drive, an external hard disk or another machine on your network if you have one. Alternatively, you could use the Transfer Wizard.

Drivers

Check that you have driver or installation disks for printers, modem, etc. and download anything you need (or may need) from manufacturers' websites.

Settings

You should write down the settings that you need to access the Internet and to send and receive email. Your user name and password for Internet access will probably be with the documentation that you received when the connection was first set up. If you can't find what you need, a phone call or an email to the support staff at you Internet Service Provider (ISP) should do the trick. If you have lost your password, they will not be able to recover it for you, but providing that you can prove who you are, they can probably reset it for you.

Your key email settings are: your user name, password and server addresses. You may be able to obtain these from your email provider (as often as not this will be your ISP) either by a call or an email to their Help Desk or by visiting their website and looking for a 'settings' page. In addition to your user name and password for email, you will also need the addresses of two mail servers which are used for sending and receiving email. For most users these are in the form of:

> pop3.yourisp.com (for incoming mail)

and

> smtp.yourisp.com (for outgoing mail)

Depending on your provider, these servers may have slightly different names like mail.yourisp.com or relay.yourisp.com – check with your service provider or dig around in your email program to find the information that you need.

To find your email settings in Outlook Express:

1 Start the program by clicking on its icon.

2 Open the **Tools** menu and select **Accounts**. This will take you to the Internet Accounts dialog box. Click on the Mail tab. This will show you your email accounts (Figure 13.04).

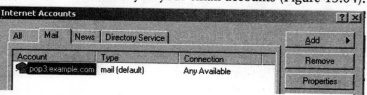

Figure 13.04

3 Highlight the email account that you wish to examine and click on **Properties**. This will take you to a dialog box as in Figure 13.05, which shows you your email settings. Write them down.

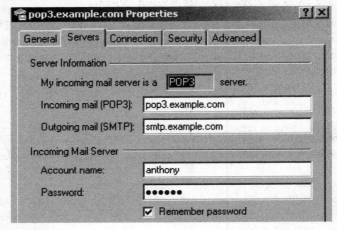

Figure 13.05

Note: if you are using Windows Mail in Vista, the procedures outlined above for XP's Outlook Express are almost identical.

13.3 The Files and Settings Transfer Wizard

(Easy Transfer Wizard in Vista)

Windows XP versions provide a utility called the Files and Settings Transfer Wizard which is intended to make it easy to migrate between systems – its equivalent in Vista is the Easy Transfer Wizard. You can use one of these wizards to back up all files and settings prior to a reinstall. The main problem with this is the sheer volume of data that you back up – it all has to be stored away from the PC, either on removable storage or a network drive. If you have a working backup system in place, all you need is to use this to make an up-to-date backup of your data files and leave only the (relatively small) backup of settings to the Wizard. Even so, it may still be wise to make a note of key settings like passwords and mail addresses on paper.

To start the wizard:

1 Open the **Start** menu, point to **All Programs** then **Accessories** then **System Tools** and select **Files and Settings Transfer Wizard** (XP) or **Easy Transfer Wizard** (Vista).

We will carry on with XP Files and Transfer Wizard. This works similarly in both Home and Professional editions. The Vista version is broadly similar, though if anything, it is even easier to use!

2 At the Welcome Screen – click **Next**. You will be asked if this is the New computer or the Old computer.

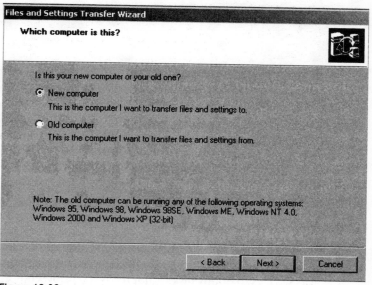

Files and Settings Transfer Wizard

Which computer is this?

Is this your new computer or your old one?

○ New computer

This is the computer I want to transfer files and settings to.

○ Old computer

This is the computer I want to transfer files and settings from.

Note: The old computer can be running any of the following operating systems: Windows 95, Windows 98, Windows 98SE, Windows ME, Windows NT 4.0, Windows 2000 and Windows XP (32-bit)

< Back | Next > | Cancel

Figure 13.06

3 The default value for the wizard is **New** – change this to **Old** and click **Next**. You will now have to wait for a minute or two while the wizard gathers information about your system before moving to the next screen which asks you to select a transfer method. The default – Direct cable on the Serial Port – requires you to have a spare computer available to make your backup over a temporary connection. This option is one which many people find troublesome and it is, quite frankly, more trouble than it is worth. If you have a home

network, you can choose to backup over your network. If you only have a stand-alone PC, then you can backup to a folder on that machine before transferring it to a removable device or a series of floppy disks.

4 If you choose the floppy disk option and click **Next**, the default action on the next screen is to backup only your settings – these may well fit on a single floppy disk.

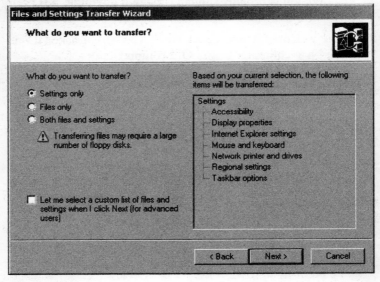

Figure 13.07

5 Click **Next** to back up your settings to the floppy disk in drive A:. Note the warning in Figure 13.07 – backing up files as well as settings to floppy disks is not really a sensible choice.

Figure 13.08

6   The alternative to using floppy disks is a removable drive or a network drive. If you select this option, you can browse to any location on your PC – such as a removable disk or pen drive, or you may navigate to another PC on your network. There is also an option to create a new folder on your target drive to hold your transferred data and settings.

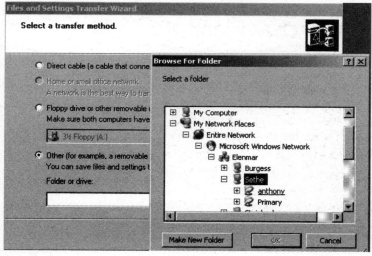

Figure 13.09

7   With your new storage area selected, click **Next** and choose whether to backup files and settings or settings only, then click **Next** to start the backup.

8   With your backup made and the backup disk removed, or disconnected and all your information gathered and stored, it's time for a final check before starting the reinstall.

A final check

Whatever method, or combination of methods you used, you should now have a backup of key information from your PC:

+   data
+   drivers
+   settings.

With this information gathered and safely stored you are ready to begin the relatively straightforward process of installing Windows. Depending on your system this may require you to use a Restore disk from the PC manufacturer – an OEM install – or you may need to use a branded Microsoft installation disk – a conventional install. We will look at both methods in turn.

13.4 An OEM install

OEM stands for *Original Equipment Manufacturer*. This term does not indicate the manufacturers of the various components, but the system builder who assembled them into a PC. System builders – particularly the large ones like Dell, or Compaq – often have a licensing agreement with Microsoft to supply a pre-installed version of Windows which is specific to that make and model of PC.

This type of OEM version of Windows is usually provided on one (or more) CDs which are labelled something like System Restore disks. They contain an image of the installed system and are flashed onto the hard drive in order to restore your PC to the state that it was in when it left the factory. When you run a Restore of this type, you will restore the operating system along with any other pre-installed software that may have been bundled with the system when you bought it. This is a rather inflexible approach, but it has the advantage of being very easy to do.

The first thing to do is to read the instructions! Although there are generic similarities between Restore disks there may be differences of detail between different manufacturers. Generally speaking, however, unless the instructions from the manufacturer state otherwise, put the Restore disk in the CD-ROM drive on your PC, restart the PC and follow the instructions on screen.

Depending on the speed of your system, the largely automated process of restoring the system may take anything up to an hour. When you are finished, remove the Restore disk and put it somewhere safe – you may need it again one day. Having done this, you will need to restore your backed-up data and settings. See the *Post Install* section below.

13.5 A conventional install

Checking CMOS/BIOS settings

Before you start an install there are a couple of things worth checking in the CMOS setup utility. *How to access the BIOS/CMOS settings* in Chapter 6 describes how to do this.

Once you are in the setup utility, you are interested in two items: the boot order of the PC and the status of CMOS anti-virus checking. Both of these settings can be important for the install process.

If there is an anti-virus function in the CMOS setup and it is set to Enabled, then change it to Disabled. The reason is that the Windows Installer will write to system areas of your hard disk as part of the installation process and this could look like virus activity to the anti-virus utility.

The boot order is the order in which the system looks at the various drives as it starts up. To boot to, and install from, a CD or DVD disk, the boot order in CMOS needs to be set so that the system looks at the CD or DVD drive first. Figure 13.10 shows how this is done in a setup screen for a Phoenix BIOS.

Figure 13.10

To navigate within the setup utility you will need to use the arrow keys to move the cursor (there's no mouse support in most CMOS setup utilities) and other keys as instructed in the 'Help' screens. Here, we use the left and right arrow keys to move along the menu at the top and the up and down ones to move up and down the menus. In the example in Figure 13.10, the CDROM drive is second in the list on the Boot menu. To make it first in the list, navigate to it using the arrow keys then, when it is highlighted, press [+] to move it up the list. Any item in the list may be promoted with [+] or demoted with [-]. When you have set the boot order to what you want – in this case CD-ROM, Hard Drive, Removable drive would be ideal – exit from the setup program and save your changes.

Other BIOS manufacturers use their own interfaces to the setup utility, so if you have (say) an AMI or AWARD BIOS they will have the facility to change the boot order but they may use entirely different ways of achieving it. Experiment – and don't forget the Quit without saving option if you get yourself into a mess!

Starting the installer

Before you start the install, check that you have the necessary product key to install Windows – the disk's packaging should have the *Product Key* on the back. This is a 25-character code in the form:

XXXXX-XXXXX-XXXXX-XXXXX-XXXXX

You will need it to complete the installation process.

Installing XP Home Edition

1 To start the installation process, put the installation disk in the CD or DVD drive and restart your PC. The system will detect the disk and prompt you to 'Press any key' to start the installer. When you do this, the display turns from white-on-black to white-on-blue and the system takes a minute or two to load various drivers. When this is done you will see a 'Welcome' screen – white text on a blue background – something like the one in Figure 13.11.

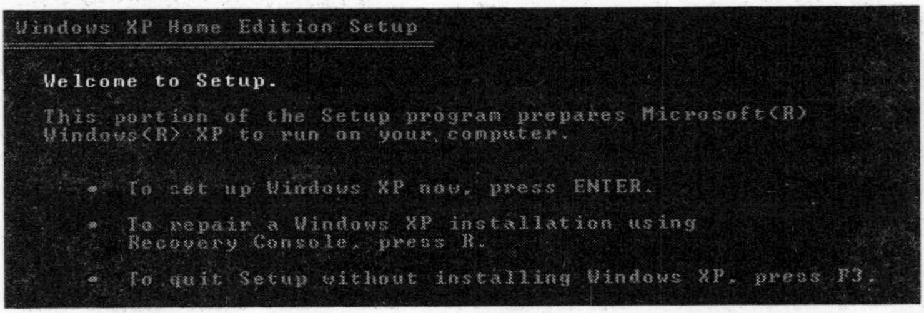

Figure 13.11

2 Press [**Enter**] to continue with the installation. The system displays the End User License Agreement (EULA) – Figure 13.12 shows the first few lines of this. Press [**F8**] to accept the terms of the EULA and to proceed with the installation.

Figure 13.12

3 The next stage of the installation process is to partition and format your hard disk. If this is a clean install on to a new disk the system will show you the amount of free space on the disk and you can install on to this just by accepting default values – i.e. use the whole of the free space and format it with the NTFS file system.

4 If, as in this example, you are doing a reinstall, the system will show you the existing setup.

5 In this example, we have a previous installation that we want to remove prior to a new one. Press [**D**] to delete this partition. You will receive a warning notice that you are about to remove a system partition – this is what you want to do, so confirm this by pressing [**Enter**].

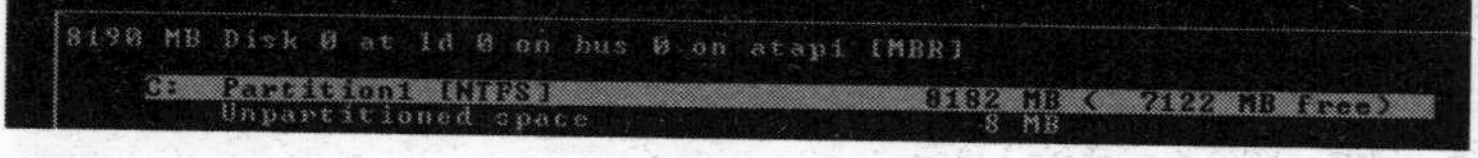

Figure 13.13

6 You will be asked to confirm (again) that you want to do this, by pressing [**L**], followed by [**Enter**] to install on the newly created free space.

```
Windows XP Home Edition Setup

You asked Setup to delete the partition
   C:  Partition1 [NTFS]                        8182 MB ( 7122 MB free)
on 8190 MB Disk 0 at Id 0 on bus 0 on atapi [MBR].

   •   To delete this partition, press L.
       CAUTION: All data on this partition will be lost.
   •   To return to the previous screen without
       deleting the partition, press ESC.
```

Figure 13.14

7 This takes you to another screen where you will be asked for
   format options as shown in Figure 13.15. The default choice
   is to use the NTFS file system. Press [Enter] to accept this.
   The system will display a progress bar as it runs the format.
   Depending on your disk size, and the overall power of your
   PC this may be several minutes' work – probably enough
   time to make a cup of tea or coffee!

```
Windows XP Home Edition Setup

A new partition for Windows XP has been created on

8190 MB Disk 0 at Id 0 on bus 0 on atapi [MBR].

This partition must now be formatted.

From the list below, select a file system for the new partition.
Use the UP and DOWN ARROW keys to select the file system you want,
and then press ENTER.

If you want to select a different partition for Windows XP,
press ESC.

   Format the partition using the NTFS file system (Quick)
   Format the partition using the FAT file system (Quick)
   Format the partition using the NTFS file system
   Format the partition using the FAT file system
```

Figure 13.15

8 When the format is complete, the installer copies files to your
   hard disk – again this can be a lengthy process – time enough
   to drink the cuppa that you made in the previous step. This
   copying is monitored and reported by another progress bar.

```
Setup is formatting...
                              100%
```

Figure 13.16

Once file copying is finished, for the remainder of the process the system moves to a graphical interface, which keeps

you informed about progress and even gives estimates of the time remaining before completion. Treat these estimates with caution.

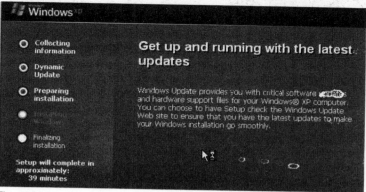

Figure 13.17

9 The next stage which requires input from you is the choice of language settings. The default is the United States. To change this, click **Customize...**

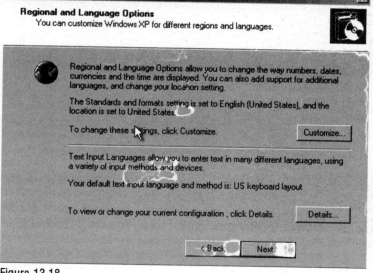

Figure 13.18

10 Choose the country settings (UK if that's where you live) for Standard and formats, and Location as shown in Figure 13.19.

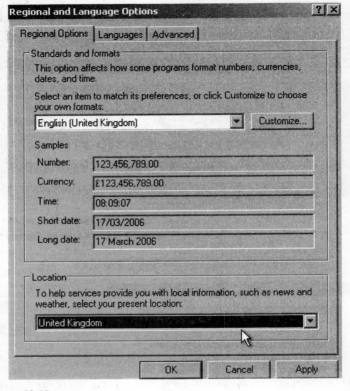

Figure 13.19

11 You should also set the default language and keyboard input options by clicking **Details** near the bottom right of the dialog box, as shown back in Figure 13.18.

12 With these details entered and confirmed, continue with the installation by clicking **Next**. You will be prompted to enter a user name – which is mandatory – and an organization name which is optional. Enter a name and click **Next** to continue. You will be prompted to enter the 25-character product key. Enter this carefully, as shown in Figure 13.20.

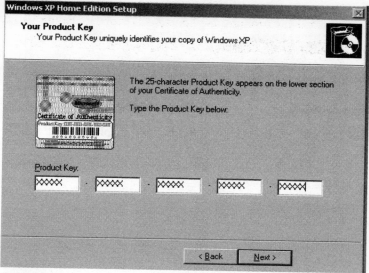

Figure 13.20

13 Click **Next** to continue the installation. If you have made a mistake you will see an error message. If this happens, you can go back and correct it.

14 The next stage is to give your PC a name – this is optional, but something meaningful or attractive is probably better that the system-generated name.

15 Having named the computer – or accepting the default – click **Next** and you will be prompted to enter your Time Zone. You can also check (and change if necessary) the current time and date information for your PC.

16 With this information in place the installer sets up your network settings. Accept the default Typical Settings option and click **Next** to continue. The installer will now run for some time. It requires no further input from you until after it has rebooted itself.

17 After the system has rebooted itself you will probably be prompted to adjust your display settings as shown in Figure 13.21.

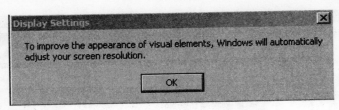

Figure 13.21

18 Click **OK** to accept this. Windows will display the XP splash screen while it works in the background before taking you to the Welcome screen and inviting you to spend a few minutes setting up your computer.

Figure 13.22

19 You can now step through the Internet Connection options – or you can skip this step and come back to it later. Chapter 15 covers the topic of connecting to the Internet if you want to read up on it.

20 The next stage is activating the product over the Internet. This is an anti-piracy feature which checks that the installation is from a properly licensed copy of Windows which has not previously been installed on a *different* machine – you are allowed to install it as many times as you like on this, your original machine.

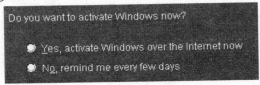

Figure 13.23

21 You can activate the product now or wait – choose the appropriate radio button to do this. If you wait, you will be reminded to do so from time to time. You have 30 days to activate so there's no hurry. Whichever choice you make, click on **Next** to continue.

22 The next screen prompts you to enter names of people who will be using the PC in order to set up user accounts for them. This is something that you can do now if you wish, or you can create additional user accounts through the Windows Control Panel at a later date.

23 When you have finished adding users to the system, click on **Next** and you will be shown the Welcome screen which lists the names of the users you have created.

Figure 13.24

24 Just click on a name and you are ready to go!

13.6 Post-install

If you used the Files and Settings Transfer Wizard/Easy Transfer Wizard to back up your settings or your data and settings, now is the time to run it.

1 Navigate to the Wizard in the System Tools and start it.

2 Click **Next** in the Welcome screen. The next screen asks whether this is the New or the Old computer. Accept the default value of New and click **Next**.

3 Because you have already backed up the settings (or files and settings) from the Old computer – i.e. the old setup before

you reinstalled – change the radio button to the I don't need...
option as shown in Figure 13.26, then click **Next**.

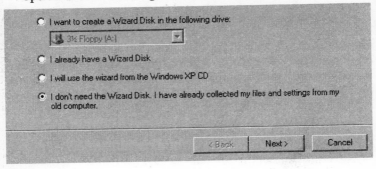

○ I want to create a Wizard Disk in the following drive:

  3½ Floppy (A:)

○ I already have a Wizard Disk

○ I will use the wizard from the Windows XP CD

◉ I don't need the Wizard Disk. I have already collected my files and settings from my
old computer.

< Back   Next >   Cancel

Figure 13.25

4 The next screen asks you to indicate where the backed up
data/settings are located. If you saved your files and settings
to another drive, e.g. a CD or a network drive, use the *Browse*
option to navigate to it.

5 If you only backed up your settings to a floppy disk, click the
appropriate radio button and put the floppy with the saved
information into the disk drive and follow the instructions.

6 If, for any reason, the Wizard fails (and they often do!) or
you chose to back up your files and settings manually, you
will need to restore them manually. The exact order in which
you do this isn't particularly important. You may restore your
files from the backup medium and then do the settings or
you may chose to reinstate your settings first.

7 To restore your files, run the Restore option of whatever
backup method you used to save them. This may be simply
copying from removable media such as a CD or a pen drive,
or you may have used the backup facilities provided with
Windows. Whatever your backup system, now is the time to
put its Restore facilities to the test. You may want to refer
back to Chapter 6, *Backup strategies*, to remind yourself of
the details.

8 With your data files restored, you need to restore your other
settings – particularly the settings needed to connect to the
Internet and email servers.

9 To connect to the Internet you will probably need to reinstall your modem. If you have a setup disk from the supplier, use it. If you need to do this by hand, skip forward to Chapter 15, *The Internet and email*, and follow the instructions for your modem type. You will need your user name and password for this – *that's* why you wrote them down – old fashioned ink on paper instead of trusting a Wizard!

10 With your Internet connection in place and working, you will need to set up your email program. Again, if you wrote down the settings on paper, this is easy enough to do. Figures 13.05 and 13.06 walked you through the process of collecting this information from Outlook Express – all you now need to do is to restore them. If you are using a different email program, such as Outlook or Pegasus or the increasingly popular (and free) Thunderbird you will have to dig around in the interface to restore your settings.

11 With Internet connectivity and email restored, this may be a good time to run the Windows Update service – there have probably been a lot of critical updates since you bought your PC and they will have been lost in the process of reinstalling.

12 There are several ways of running the Windows Update service. Any of the following should work:

   ◆ Type *wupdmgr* at a system prompt or in a Run box (XP).

   ◆ If you use Internet Explorer, choose the **Update** option from the **Tools** menu.

   ◆ Point your browser to **windowsupdate.microsoft.com**.

   ◆ Use the menu command **Start > All Programs > Windows update**.

13 Once you are at the Windows Update site, just follow the instructions on screen to update your system. You may also want to look back to page 53 to remind yourself about automatic updates.

14 If you are running XP and your version does not have Service Pack 2 incorporated in it, then the Automatic Updates will install it piecemeal. If you prefer, you can download a copy of Service Pack 2 for XP from the Microsoft website. It is a

simple installer program – just click on the icon and follow the instructions. When the installer has finished – and it can be quite a long job – you will be prompted to reboot your PC. After that you will be prompted to configure the Security Center which is one of the Service Pack 2 enhancements. The Security Center is described in Chapter 2, *System tools*.

15 The final essential task is to reinstall your applications programs and tweaking Windows – refer back to Chapter 12, *Components and programs*, if you have any doubts about how to go about this.

Two final optional tasks may be to defragment your hard disk and manually set a system restore point. Installer programs use a lot of temporary files as they work and delete them when they finish, often leaving a badly fragmented disk and even leftover temporary files. Setting a system restore point, can also save a lot of driver reinstalling, etc. should you need to make changes in the next day or so.

This may be a good time to go back to Chapter 1, *Maintaining Windows*.

Summary

This chapter has looked at the process of installing or reinstalling Windows. Whether you undertake an OEM install or a conventional one, it is not difficult. However, reinstalling Windows removes *everything* from your hard disk, so we have looked at how to prepare for a reinstall by backing up files and settings, and how to restore them. We have looked at the Files and Settings Transfer Wizard for doing this and have considered alternative ways of going about things.

When they work, wizards can save you a certain amount of time and effort, but if they go wrong, you end up with all your data in an obscure proprietary file format that you can't read. Even if you intend to use a wizard for an operation, it is probably wise to have normal backups of your files and to write down critical settings such as user names, passwords and email details – if you have these, you can at least access the Internet and get some help.

14 troubleshooting

In this chapter you will learn:

- how to gather the facts: observe, use diagnostic utilities, ask the user

- how to make a list of the possibilities, then work through it testing and noting results

14.1 General guidelines

Sooner or later you will be faced with a machine that just won't work. You will have tried everything that you can think of, looked at the manuals and emailed your friends, but still, it just won't work. What's needed now, is not an encyclopaedia of PC problems (which would have to be a very big book to list all of them!) but a systematic approach to fault diagnosis.

Using Device Manager

All Windows versions have a utility called Device Manager. It is by no means perfect, but if you have a working – or nearly working – Windows system, the Device Manager can be a good place to start your enquiries.

To start Device Manager:

1   Right-click on *(My) Computer* and select **Properties** from the context menu.

2   Choose the **Hardware** tab, then click **Device Manager**.

Figure 14.01

Figure 14.01 shows the Device Manager output for a system called ASIMOV which has a problem with a network adaptor. The list of these is open and the suspect device is highlighted.

In this instance, the device has simply been disabled. Right-clicking on the item in the list and selecting **Enable** from the context menu is sufficient to fix the problem.

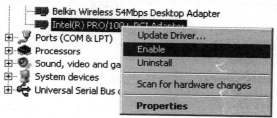

Figure 14.02

Windows enables the device and redraws the output of Device Manager to show a closed-up list for the section that had been reporting a problem.

As you can see from Figure 14.02, the context menu for a device reported as having a problem includes several other trouble-shooting options such as reinstalling the drivers for the device or uninstalling it from the system. Whatever option you try from this menu will, if it successfully solves the problem, result in a closed-up list in Device Manager.

If you can't effect a cure through Device Manager or – uncommon but not unknown – the non-functioning device is reported as working when it is not, you may have to start working directly with the hardware and Operating System components. The key to success in this is a systematic approach.

14.2 Isolating the symptom

The modern multimedia PC is a complex machine. It has many items of hardware (usually from different manufacturers) as well as applications software, device driver software, and so on. The key to successful fault diagnosis is the systematic examination of these in order to isolate and fix the problem.

When diagnosing hardware problems, this usually means removing suspect hardware components one at a time until the problem rights itself. Using this method the last component removed is probably the defective part. Alternatively, some technicians will strip a PC down to its components and reassemble it from first principles, testing each stage of the build as they go. This can be quite a challenge for the home user, but it may be worth the effort. Experience has shown that a radical rebuild will sometimes cause a problem to disappear even though you never found out the exact cause – there are so many components, so many possibilities for a bad contact between components that a rebuild is quicker than testing every possible bad connection individually.

In terms of software diagnosis, the process is essentially similar – remove any programs that may be running in the background – disconnect from the Internet and turn off your virus checker and firewall, for example – until only the suspect program is running. If, at this stage, the problem persists, try uninstalling the suspect software package. In XP use Control Panel > Add/ Remove Programs (in Vista use Control Panel > Programs > Installed Programs) and remove the suspect application. After you have done this – rebooting the machine if necessary – reinstall your application from the original disk. If this fixes the problem – fine. Just don't forget to restart your firewall and virus scanner before reconnecting to the Internet!

With both software and hardware diagnosis, you are making a list – formally on paper or just in your own mind – then working systematically through it, eliminating possibilities in order to isolate and fix the problem.

14.3 Separating software from hardware

It is not always easy to tell if a problem is caused by a hardware or a software fault, so there are a handful of things which most technicians find useful.

- Known good hardware. If you have a suitable replacement component that is 'known good' – either new or borrowed from a working machine – swap the suspect part for the known good part and if this fixes the problem, then you know which component to replace. This swap out is not always easy for the home user with only one PC. Even so, if for example, you have two sticks of RAM installed and you suspect a memory problem, you can remove one stick and boot the machine using only the other. If it cures the problem, power down and swap the RAM and reboot. If the problem reappears, then you have successfully isolated it and know which RAM stick to replace. (Don't forget anti-static precautions when doing this!)

- Uninstall/reinstall – as noted earlier, uninstalling and reinstalling suspect software can often fix a problem.

- Patching and upgrading – this is particularly applicable to device drivers for hardware components. It is good practice to download patches or upgrades from manufacturers' websites, anyway, and if it helps to fix a problem then it is definitely worthwhile.

- Virus check – at some point it will be necessary to run a full system scan with an up-to-date virus scanner. If a system is functioning reasonably well, or you have reason to suspect a virus, it may be a good idea to start your investigation by running a virus scan. You may also like to run a scanner to detect ad-ware, spyware or other 'malware' at the same time. See also Chapter 16, *Viruses and other malware*.

- Common sense – no set of rules or guidelines can provide an alternative to common sense. Think carefully about the problem and make notes if necessary. Assume nothing and always – yes, *always* – look for the obvious. There is no point in testing the PC's internal power supply unit if the fuse in the plug on the wall has blown!

14.4 Investigating the problem

If you have tried the general approach outlined above and still can't find the answer to the problem, you will need to investigate further and a little more systematically. Imagine that you are working for someone else – a customer – or that you are making a call to a remote Help Desk and you are preparing to answer their probable questions.

Describe the problem

If you were to make a call to a Help Desk you would need to describe the problem to them in both general and specific terms. Go back and review Chapter 4, *Making a support call*, and step though the sections on *Defining the problem* and *Gathering the information*. This exercise will, if nothing else, help you to organize your thoughts.

This is also the time at which you should consider other users of the PC. If you share the machine with other family members – particularly children – you need to enlist their help in finding the cause of the problem. Tact and diplomacy are at least as important as technical knowledge for this undertaking. If you can approach this as simply a problem to be solved, without implying any kind of blame on anyone, you are more likely to win their co-operation and find a solution quickly.

Reproduce the problem

A problem which has only happened once isn't really a problem – it's a one-off inconvenience. The first thing to do, then, is to reboot the PC and reproduce the problem. Do this in a systematic manner, noting in particular any error messages that the system gives you. At this stage, the problem and its solution often become apparent – a missing Desktop shortcut, for example can generally be fixed either by letting Windows search for the target file, or you may want to delete the icon and make a new shortcut to your application.

Whatever, the cause, and whatever the cure, always reboot the machine and test that your fix has worked.

What has changed recently?

Another fruitful line of enquiry when troubleshooting is to ask (yourself or others) what, if anything, has changed recently. The fact is that systems which are working properly tend to go on working properly (though not always, of course!) and many failures result from changes to the system which have had unintended consequences.

Systems that have had hardware or software changes are more likely to manifest faults than those that have been chugging along quietly for some time. Hardware changes are usually fairly obvious – if you added a disk drive or fitted some more RAM yesterday and the PC is playing up today, it is a relatively simple task to reverse the changes and see if that cures the problem.

Software changes can be more difficult to detect. You may have downloaded operating system updates, device drivers or utilities and these may be conflicting with other installed programs. If someone else who uses the PC has downloaded something, this too, may be causing you problems.

If you can't track down the problem, and you suspect that it is software related you can check in Add/Remove Programs to see if there are any unfamiliar entries, including operating system updates from Microsoft which may have been downloaded and installed as Automatic Updates.

Another place worth checking is System Restore which will list all recent software updates and give you the opportunity to roll back the system to an earlier date.

Hardware problems are most likely to be visible in Device Manager (see Figures 14.01 and 14.02 above).

A recent change of hardware or software is the most likely cause of a problem but this may not necessarily be the case. For example, if you do a RAM upgrade on your PC and it boots fine afterwards, but crashes after a few minutes then the cause is almost certainly not the memory upgrade. The crash-after-five-minutes symptom is typical of an overheating CPU chip – possibly the CPU fan became disconnected from the motherboard in the course of the memory upgrade. In this case, something has changed of course, but not necessarily the most readily apparent thing.

14.5 Diagnostic utilities

Device Manager

As noted earlier in the chapter, Device Manager should probably be the first tool that you use to investigate a fault with your PC. It is, as often as not, your last – once you have fixed the problem – a Device Manager that displays a closed-up list is a good indicator that your efforts have been successful.

System Information

This is one of the System Tools which can be reached through the Start > All Programs ... route. It gives rather more detailed information than Device Manager and can be useful for tracking down problems such as conflicts between devices. It has an Explorer style interface. The default view – as in Figure 14.03 – is a System Summary. To expand the list in the left pane, click the + signs; the right pane displays the details of the item selected in the left.

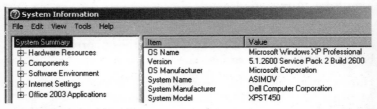

Figure 14.03

The **Tools** and **View** menus are of interest for troubleshooting purposes. The Tools menu contains some utilities which are frankly rather obscure, though you can run System Restore from here. The View menu includes History which will give you an indication of recent changes to the system.

Check Disk (CHKDSK.EXE)

CHKDSK is a disk checking utility that has been present in all Windows versions since the early days. As the name suggests it is used to check and fix various problems that may arise with your hard disk. Using CHKDSK is described in Chapter 1, as one of the 'four useful tools'. This utility can be run from the Windows Graphical User Interface (GUI) or it can be started from a command line or a Run box by typing in CHKDSK followed by [Enter].

Windows Memory Diagnostic

This is a utility from Microsoft which is not distributed with Windows itself, but which can be downloaded from their site free of charge. You can also download the instructions on how to use it from there. A search on the terms 'Windows memory diagnostic' should find the relevant page. After you have downloaded this utility – a file called MTINST.EXE – click on it to run it. You will be required to accept the standard Microsoft Licence Agreement. Accepting this will take you to a choice between creating a bootable floppy or a bootable CD-ROM. Create one or the other – or both!

Once you have created a bootable CD or floppy, put it in the appropriate drive, boot your PC to it and follow the instructions on screen to test your system RAM – this will probably take around five minutes, though the time taken will vary according to the speed of your PC and the amount of memory to be checked.

When you have finished, don't forget to remove the bootable disk from the drive before restarting your PC.

MSCONFIG – the system configuration utility

This is a diagnostic utility which has been present in all recent Windows. To start it in either version of XP, type MSCONFIG in a Run box or, in Vista, run it from a command line prompt or the Start Search box. You need Administrator rights to do this.

Many of the capabilities of MSCONFIG are beyond the needs of the home user. However, the Startup tab gives you control over which programs run at boot time.

Entries in the list which have a checked box next to them will run at boot time – those which are cleared will not. In this example, two items have been disabled. These programs are still available for use, of course, but will not run automatically at

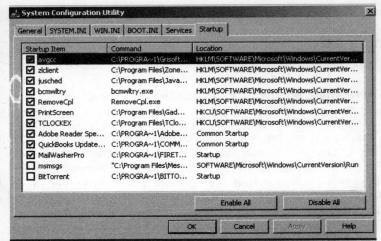

Figure 14.04

boot time. There are also buttons to enable or disable all startup options.

If you want to explore the possibilities of MSCONFIG further, clicking on the Help button will take you to an online manual for this utility. There is also a search feature within the Help system which will help you to find the information you need.

Using Safe Mode

Safe Mode is a diagnostic mode of operation for Windows which has a minimal set of software drivers. Using Safe Mode is described in section 1.4, page 13.

Third-party tools

In addition to the tools provided with Windows there are third-party utilities which are frequently used by system builders and field engineers. One of the best known of these is PC-Check from Eurosoft. This is a fairly expensive (but good) professional tool. Other proprietary diagnostic software utilities are available.

14.6 Some common problems and their solutions

Most hardware errors are caused either by failure of a component or by some type of connection problem. Before trying anything else, open the PC case, remove and reseat the suspect component and check that, where necessary, it has power and that any data cable or connector is correctly fitted. Reboot the PC. This is frequently sufficient to cure a problem.

When you have ruled out this sort of simple connectivity problem, remove the component and, if possible, try it in another PC if you have access to one. If it doesn't work in another PC, chances are that it is dead and needs to be replaced. Alternatively, try a new component of the correct type in your PC. For a really cheap item, such as a floppy drive, the cost of simply buying a new component in order to do this is minimal.

Most software or operating system problems are caused by wrong settings or a virus attack.

Table 14.01 (page 206) is not an exhaustive list, just an indication of some of the most frequently encountered PC problems. Some viruses will mimic hardware failures, so if the PC is functioning sufficiently well a virus scan may be a good first step in the troubleshooting process.

Summary

This chapter has introduced you to the methods that PC technicians and field engineers use when diagnosing faults. They key thing is to approach the investigation in a systematic way. Ask questions – of yourself and other users of the PC. Ask questions of the PC itself, using utilities such as System Information, Device Manager and CHKDSK. If necessary, remove suspect hardware or software and test the results. Make a list of the possibilities and work through it systematically and patiently. Don't lose your nerve, don't lose your temper – the problem can be fixed and there's a good chance that you can fix it.

Table 14.01 Common symptoms and solutions

Symptom	Probable cause/solution
System loses time and date settings	Weak or dead CMOS battery. Fit a new battery and update CMOS settings as needed.
Won't boot to floppy or CD-ROM	Check that the disk is in fact bootable – floppies in particular, easily become corrupted or damaged. Check physical connections – data and power cables. Check the 'boot order' using the CMOS 'Setup' utility.
Keyboard errors	Check physical connection to the PC. Check for stuck keys. Check that you have the correct keyboard. See *Regional and Language Settings*, page 41.
Intermittent boot failures	These are usually caused by: A failing power supply unit. See *Replacing a power supply unit*, page 107. A virus. Run a virus check, see Chapter 16, *Viruses* ...
System starts, runs for few minutes, then crashes	Typical of an overheating problem. Power down, open the case and check that all fans work when you power up again. Check for excessive build-up of dust on heat sinks.
Memory errors	Power down and open the case. Reseat RAM modules. Reboot. If the problem persists run memory diagnostics and replace any RAM found to be faulty.
Won't read a drive	Check cabling and power. Check for presence of removable media in the case of CD/DVD or tape. Test with known good media. Check CMOS settings. Test the drive in another machine. For parallel ATA drives check master/slave jumper settings.
Display problems	Usually caused by wrong settings. Check the Display settings, see page 38. You may need to boot to Safe Mode to do this if the display is unreadable.
Sound/speakers	Check cable connections. Check volume settings in both hardware and software. Look in Device Manager for resource conflicts/driver problems.
Modems	Check cable connections. Check passwords and user names. Check that the phone line is working.

15

the internet and email

In this chapter you will learn:

- how to set up your Internet connection

- how to configure your web browser

- how firewalls work

- how email works

15.1 How to set up your Internet connection

Connecting to the Internet – for surfing, shopping, online banking, sending and receiving emails – is one of the main uses for the Home PC.

Before you start

In order to connect to the Internet you need some form of access account with an Internet Service Provider (ISP) and a physical connection through a modem or a router. To set up your Internet connection you will need an active account with your ISP, who will have provided you with a user name and a password – make sure you have these to hand.

Many ISPs provide a broadband modem as part of their broadband package. If this is the case, check that you have all the necessary cables and connectors and that you have read any installation instructions that come with it.

If you have bought your own modem (or router) you should also check any documentation that came with it. This chapter will take you through the setup process for equipment of this type though details may vary between specific products.

Installing a USB broadband modem

The most popular way of connecting to the Internet is through some form of broadband connection – this is also known as an Asymmetric Digital Subscriber Line (ADSL) connection. As we will see in Chapter 17, *Home networking*, this type of modem connection can be shared over a home network. For the time being, however, we will look at the process of installing a fairly typical broadband modem for a single PC.

The modem used in this example is from Alcatel and it connects to a USB port. As with most USB devices it is necessary to install device drivers before attaching the hardware.

1 Put the installation CD in the drive. It should autorun. If it doesn't, navigate to the CD drive through My Computer and

click on the icon. You will see a Welcome screen like the one in Figure 15.01.

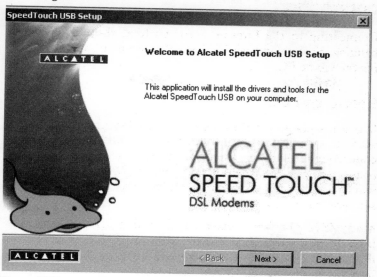

Figure 15.01

2   Click **Next** to move on, then click **Yes** to accept the licence agreement for the software, then **Next** again to start the installation. The default install is to your C: drive – accept this.

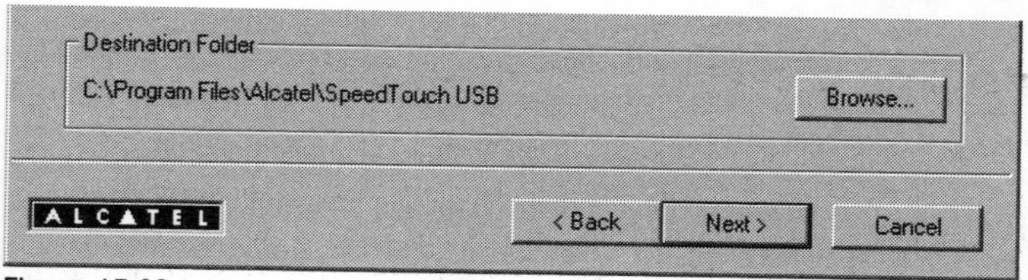

Figure 15.02

3   Click **Next** again and the installer will start copying files to your hard disk.

4   You may see a warning about unsigned drivers. Providing you are installing from a manufacturer's disk supplied with the modem, or downloaded from their site, it is safe to click **Continue anyway**. After a few seconds the installer will complete its work and you will be advised that you may now

connect your modem to the PC. Plug it in to one of the USB ports, then click **Finish**.

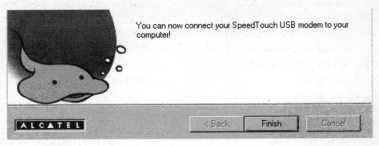

Figure 15.03

5 The Found New Hardware Wizard will ask you if you want to connect to Windows Update.

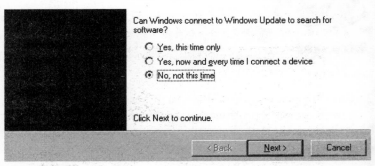

Figure 15.04

6 You don't need to do this, as you have installed the drivers from the manufacturer's disk. Choose **No** and click **Next**. At the next screen choose **Install the software automatically**.

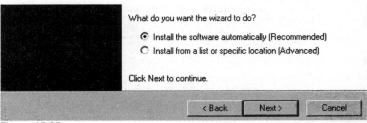

Figure 15.05

7 Click **Next** and the system will start the next stage of the installation process. When it has finished, click the **Finish** button. The installer will now run *again* – select **No, not this time** again (as in Figure 15.04) and click **Next**, then **Next** again on the screen that follows. Once again, if you receive a warning about unsigned drivers, select **Continue anyway**. When the installer is finished, click on **Finish** to close it. You will now have a modem icon on your Desktop.

8 In order to connect to the Internet, plug the cable from the modem into the ADSL splitter which is attached to the phone socket – this is an adaptor which enables you to use both modem and phone at the same time. It has two sockets – one for the phone and the other for the modem; they are different sizes and they are usually labelled *DSL* and *Phone* so that you won't confuse them.

9 To finish the process, click on the Desktop icon and enter your user name and password as in Figure 15.06.

Figure 15.06

10 Click **Connect** and – provided you have supplied the correct user name and password – you will connect to the Internet. Windows will remember the user name and password for you so that all you will need to do in future will be to click on the Desktop icon to make a connection.

11 If you can't connect to the Internet, check your user name and password, then check physical cable connections and that the phone line is working. If it still won't work, then uninstall the drivers, reboot and start again.

15.2 Installing a broadband modem/ router

An increasingly popular way of connecting to the Internet is through a combined broadband modem/router. These are standalone devices which are permanently connected to the Internet even when your PC is turned off. They often provide wireless network connectivity as well, and are ideal for use with a small home network – whether wired, wireless, or both.

The example that follows assumes that you have a working Ethernet port on your machine – most modern machines do. If you don't have a network connection – for an RJ-45 plug or a wireless card – you will need to install one. Fitting a PCI Expansion card is described in Chapter 8, and there is a description of installing a wireless Network Interface Card (NIC) in Chapter 17.

In this chapter we will look at how to set up a modem/router through the browser on a single PC and return to the networking aspects in Chapter 17.

In order to do this, it's useful for you to know a couple of things about network addresses.

Network addresses

A network address is a series of numbers, like a phone number, which identifies a node such as a PC or a router on a network. The rules for these numbers are part of the Internet Protocol and are known as Internet Protocol addresses. This is invariably shortened to IP address. An IP address consists of four groups of numbers, separated by full stops.

192.168.2.1 – is a typical private IP address. Private addresses are reserved for use on private networks – like home networks – rather than the public addresses used on the (public) Internet.

Just as a phone number may consist of an exchange code and the individual's phone number, an IP address has two parts. In the case of a typical Class C address that you will use for home networking, the first three groups of numbers are the network part of the address and the last group indicates the computer, or router, or other device attached to that network. The address 192.168.2.1, then indicates device number 1 on the network indicated by 192.168.2.

Settings and equipment check

As with all equipment installation you should check that you have all necessary cables and connectors and that you have read any instructions from the manufacturer. You will need to know some settings which will be provided by your ISP. These are:

- User name: yourusername@yourisp
- Password: nnnnnnn.

Other settings you may need for your router.

- Encapsulation: PPPoA
- Multiplexing: VC Based
- VPI: 0
- VCI: 38.

(Note: these are UK settings – if you are not in the UK, they may be different in your country/region.)

You don't need to know what these settings mean – just have them to hand and enter them when – or if – necessary.

The other thing that you will need is the router's default IP address – this will be in its manual or setup instructions. The default IP address in this example is 192.168.2.1 – this may be different if you are using a different make or model of router/modem.

Connecting your router

1   Connect all cables. There will be one from the Ethernet port on your PC to one of the ports on the router, and another from the router to the splitter which connects it and the phone to the phone line. Connect the router to its power supply. Various lights on the router will flicker as it runs through its power-on self-test/boot sequence.

2   When the router has settled down you will have an indicator to show that it is powered up along with other indicators for the ADSL side of the connection. The port to which you have connected the Ethernet cable should have a steady light to show that it is in place. Ports which have no cable attached will not show lights. If there are any problems at this stage – unlikely – then check cable connections and power and have a look at the router manual or setup instructions.

3   The next thing to do is to configure the modem/router through its web interface. To do this, start your web browser and type in the default IP address of your router. You don't need 'http' or 'www' – just type the numeric IP address in the Address bar and press [Enter].

4   The browser will add the http:// prefix for you and you will be taken to the login screen for the router. As this is the first time you have accessed the router there won't be a password in place – or if there is, it will be a default password from the manufacturer which will be shown in the documentation. The login screen will look something like Figure 15.07.

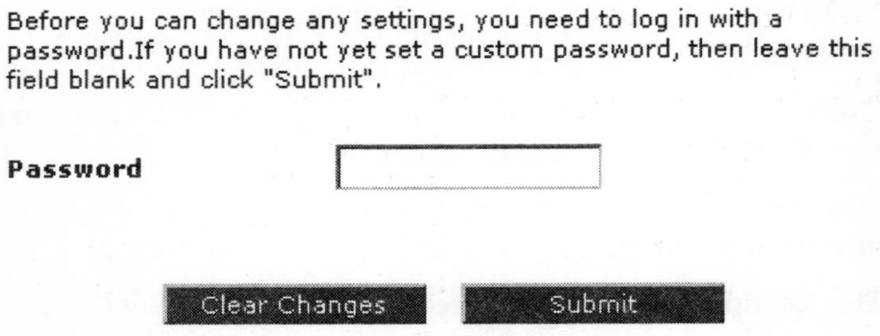

Before you can change any settings, you need to log in with a password. If you have not yet set a custom password, then leave this field blank and click "Submit".

Password

Clear Changes   Submit

Figure 15.07

5 Enter a password – if necessary – and press [Enter]. The Welcome screen will list various options, including a button for a setup wizard.

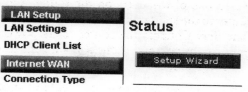

LAN Setup
LAN Settings
DHCP Client List
Internet WAN
Connection Type

Status

Setup Wizard

Figure 15.08

6 Click on this and step through the setup options one by one, entering the information from your ISP as necessary. In this example, the default Connection Type is PPPoE – change it to PPPoA (the Encapsulation setting) as shown in Figure 15.09 and click **Next**.

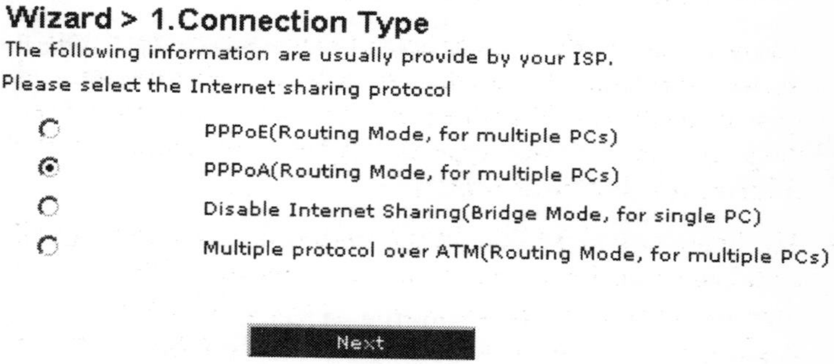

Wizard > 1.Connection Type

The following information are usually provide by your ISP.

Please select the Internet sharing protocol

○　　　　　PPPoE(Routing Mode, for multiple PCs)

◉　　　　　PPPoA(Routing Mode, for multiple PCs)

○　　　　　Disable Internet Sharing(Bridge Mode, for single PC)

○　　　　　Multiple protocol over ATM(Routing Mode, for multiple PCs)

Next

Figure 15.09

7 At the next screen enter your user name and password and the values for VPI/VCI as supplied by your ISP.

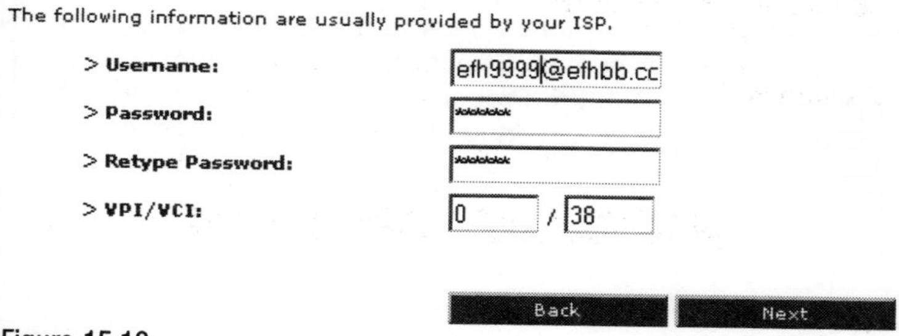

The following information are usually provided by your ISP.

> **Username:**　　　　　efh9999@efhbb.cc

> **Password:**　　　　　✱✱✱✱✱✱✱

> **Retype Password:**　　✱✱✱✱✱✱✱

> **VPI/VCI:**　　　　　0　/　38

Back　　　　Next

Figure 15.10

8 Click **Next** to continue. The Wizard will show you a summary screen.

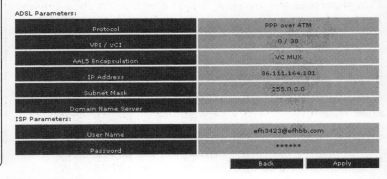

ADSL Parameters:

Protocol	PPP over ATM
VPI / VCI	0 / 38
AAL5 Encapsulation	VC MUX
IP Address	86.111.164.101
Subnet Mask	255.0.0.0
Domain Name Server	

ISP Parameters:

User Name	efh3423@efhbb.com
Password	******

Back   Apply

Figure 15.11

9 Check that the information is correct, then click **Apply**. The router will save your settings and reboot – this may take half a minute or so. Your router should now be working. Check by pointing your browser at a website.

10 This may be a good time to go back to the configuration utility and check other system settings – these will include some options such as blocking PING requests from the Internet which we will consider later when we look at firewalls. The setting that you need to fix now is simply the password to access the router configuration screens – having set it up, you don't want any one messing with it – do you?

If your browser won't connect

If your browser can't see the router, then it is probably a problem with the network settings on your PC. Navigate to the Network Connections applet in the Control Panel, and right-click on Properties. Select the Internet Protocol item in the list and click the Properties button. Make sure that your PC is set up to obtain an IP address automatically.

15.3 Setting up a dialup connection

Dialup connections are slow, but almost universally available. Unlike a broadband connection which is tied to a phone line, a typical pay-as-you-go dialup service can generally be accessed from any phone line and is billed to the telephone account. Some people also like to have a dialup available as a fall-back service if there are problems with their ADSL connection. A dialup connection requires you to have a modem installed on your system. Many desktop machines and nearly all laptop/notebook systems have a modem built into them.

Physical connection

If you don't have a modem port on your PC you will need to fit one, either as a PCI expansion card or as an external USB or serial port device. Chapter 7 outlines how to fit a PCI card and USB is covered earlier in this chapter. The example that follows shows the process of installing an internal PCI modem.

1 Power down the PC.

2 Fit the PCI modem card in a spare PCI slot.

3 Reboot and allow it to plug and play.

4 Run **Phone and Modems** in Control Panel and check for installed modems. If, as in Figure 15.12, the modem has plugged and played, you can proceed with configuration.

5 Otherwise, click **Add** and follow the instructions on screen. Provide any necessary software drivers as needed.

Fitting an external modem to a serial port is a similar undertaking. Connect the device, allow it to plug and play where possible and provide the drivers from the manufacturer's disk when prompted.

Modem settings

Modem settings are not – as you might expect – set up through the Phone and Modems applet in the Control Panel.

1 If you are using XP, navigate to the **Network Connections** applet and run the **Create a New Connection Wizard**. (In

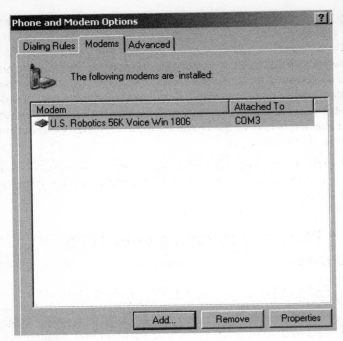

Figure 15.12

Vista, go to **Network Center** and select **Set up a connection or network** then **Set up a dialup connection**.)

Either of these wizards will take you step by step through the process of configuring your modem. The following example is taken from XP Professional – other Windows versions vary a little in detail, but are fundamentally similar.

2 Start the Wizard and accept the default choices offered until you reach the screen shown in Figure 15.13.

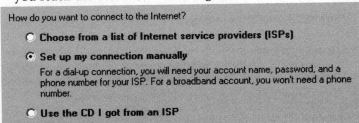

Figure 15.13

3 Change the selection to **Set up my connection manually** then click **Next**. The screens that follow will prompt you for the ISP's name, the dialup phone number, your user name and password. You will be given the opportunity to make this connection the default for the system – don't do this unless this is your only Internet connection – and to make it available to all users of the PC. Finally, you will be prompted to make a shortcut to the connection on your Desktop. Accept this, if you want one.

4 As with everything you install and configure – test that your connection works. Click on the Desktop icon and watch it dial up.

15.4 How to configure your web browser

Most home users use the Microsoft Internet Explorer web browser which is supplied with the Windows operating system. Most of the default values are suitable for most users, though there are a couple of entries that you may want to change.

1 Navigate to the configuration utility through **Control Panel > Internet Options** or **Tools > Internet Options** in Internet Explorer. Either way you will see a screen like the one in Figure 15.14 (page 220).

2 The **General** tab has most of the settings that are likely to be of use or interest to the home user. The top section allows you to change your **home page** – where the browser starts. The easy way to change this is to go to the Internet page that you want to use as 'home', then click **Use Current**.

3 The next section lets you manage **Temporary Internet files** – i.e. cookies or temporary files. Note: if you delete cookies, then sites which usually recognize you when you return to them will no longer do so, so you will have to provide log-in details again.

4 The bottom section allows you to set the number of days that your **History** of web browsing is kept on your PC. Clicking **Clear History** deletes all this information. If you do this

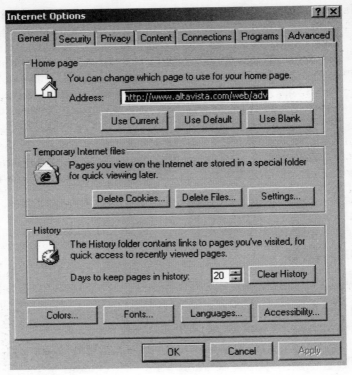

Figure 15.14

and click on the drop-down list in the browser's Address bar you will see that the list is now empty.

15.5 How firewalls work

When you connect to the Internet you are starting a two-way communication process. When you click on a link or type a web address in a browser bar you are requesting information to be sent to you. Unfortunately, there is nothing to stop anyone from sending you material that you have *not* requested. There are malicious programs which will invade your system for purposes such as data or identity theft or simply to damage your system for the sake of it.

In order to counter these threats you can use a *firewall*. This may be implemented in hardware or in software. Windows has a built-in firewall – greatly improved since the introduction of XP Service Pack 2 – or there are third-party software solutions such as Zone Alarm.

Whatever the specifics of your firewall, its basic function is that of a doorkeeper examining invitations – no invitation, no entry. When you request a page from the Internet it passes through the firewall which notes the request. When the remote site replies, the data packets which it sends are compared with the firewall's table of requests sent, and are only allowed in if they have been specifically requested by you. By default, any Windows XP PC with Service Pack 2 or later, or any version of Vista, will have this level of firewall protection implemented.

An additional level of protection is given by controlling which programs on your PC can access the Internet. Obviously, your web browser and email programs need to be given access. Other programs can be given access to the Internet if you allow them.

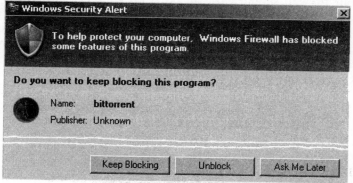

Figure 15.15

Figure 15.15 shows a program attempting to access the Internet and being intercepted by the Windows firewall. Clicking **Keep Blocking** will prevent it from accessing the Internet. Choosing **Unblock** will add the program to the list of Exceptions. If you open the firewall by clicking on the Firewall applet in the Control Panel, and click on the **Exceptions** tab you will see a list of permitted programs. You can add new programs or remove any which have previously been given Internet access.

The built-in Windows firewall is designed to give a balance between security and ease of use which is suitable for the home user. You can have greater control of your security by installing a commercial firewall product, though it may require a little more work to set up and maintain. There are a number of firewall products suitable for the home user and at least one of these – Zone Alarm – is available in a free-for-private-use version. The free version can also be upgraded to include additional features such as parental controls and anti-virus features.

If you have a home network, by the way, you only need to set up a firewall on the machine which has the direct Internet connection. Other machines which connect through this 'gateway' machine are protected by its firewall. This *does not* apply to virus protection. Each PC should have its own anti-virus software package which should be regularly updated.

Testing your firewall

Your firewall should close all ports on your PC so that they cannot be seen from the Internet. A very good – and free – service is from the Gibson Research Corporation at **www.grc.com**. Their Shields Up utility will remotely probe your PC and report any security holes which they detect. This site is also a good source of general Internet security information.

15.6 How email works

Email is one of the most widely used features of the Internet. We generally take it for granted these days that we can communicate more or less instantly with anyone in the world through email. For the home user, there are two email types – web-based services or POP3 services with addresses like yourname@yourisp.com.

Web-based services require you to log on to a site where you have an email account and everything is done whilst logged on to that site. Probably the best known web-based mail service is Microsoft's Hotmail, though there are many alternative services such as Postmaster – a UK-based service available from postmaster.co.uk.

POP3 services allow you to use a mail program such as Outlook, or Outlook Express (XP)/Windows Mail (Vista) or Thunderbird. These are all programs – known as mail clients – which allow you to compose mail off-line, then connect to the Internet to send your messages and download any that you have received. This is the mail type which is most widely used by anyone who has to deal with more than a handful of mail messages per day, though you can of course have both types of email account.

Sending and receiving POP3 emails means using two email protocols – the Post Office Protocol – version 3 (POP3), which is used for receiving emails and the Simple Mail Transfer Protocol (SMTP), which is used for sending messages from your PC. In order to set up your email client, you don't need to know anything about these mail protocols other than their names. What you do need to know, of course, is the names and addresses of the servers that use these protocols, along with your user name and password.

Chapter 4, *Making a support call*, has a section under the heading *Gathering the information* which looks at how to find (or enter) the email settings needed to make your email system work. The illustrations are of the Outlook Express mail client as this is the most popular email program with home users. It is not, however, difficult to apply the information given to other mail client programs. Just remember that you need two server addresses – possibly with the same password for each – a POP3 server for receiving incoming mail and an SMTP server for sending mail.

Summary

This chapter has looked at the basics of how to connect a single PC to the Internet and the basics of security. We have considered how to set up different modem types and how to set up a domestic modem/router.

We have examined the topic of firewalls in terms of the Windows firewall and looked at how email works.

Other aspects of security, such as virus protection and anti-spyware measures are the subject of Chapter 16.

16

viruses and other malware

In this chapter you will learn:

- how to combat viruses and other malware

- how to implement parental controls on Internet access

- what to do if you discover that you have a virus problem

16.1 Viruses, trojans and worms

If you believed all the stories you hear about the various threats that lurk on the Internet you would probably never go online again! The truth of the matter is, however, a bit less dramatic. There are some nasties around, but some sensible precautions are enough to make the risks manageable.

Viruses, trojans and worms are all types of malicious program code written with the intention of damaging some aspect of your PC's operation. They are often referred to collectively as *malware*. There are also other types of malicious code – diallers, browser hijackers, etc. – and the differences between the various nasties is not always clear, but the kind of people who write malicious code are unlikely to care too much about definitions.

16.2 Basic precautions

To keep your PC safe from attack you should download and install any security updates from Microsoft. Don't forget that if you have reinstalled Windows you will have lost all your accumulated security downloads and will have to download and install them again.

You also need a firewall of some kind. The minimum precaution is to use the Windows firewall that was bundled with Service Pack 2. If you are using a combined broadband modem/router this may also have a firewall built into it. Make sure that it is enabled. A firewall will provide basic protection from worms – such as Sasser or Netsky – which circulate on the Internet looking for vulnerable systems to exploit.

Installing and using anti-virus software

The single most important tool for dealing with virus threats is an anti-virus software package. This needs to be installed and regularly updated. Most packages can be configured to update themselves regularly and this may happen a couple of times a week. *An out-of-date virus scanner is worse than useless* – it will not protect you from the ever-evolving pool of viruses but will make you think that you are protected when you are not!

There are many anti-virus packages available and they have many similarities with each other. One of the most effective and easy to use is AVG from Grisoft. They offer a number of packages for various sizes and types of business – more importantly for the home user, they offer a free version for private use. Check that you are eligible to use the free version – if you are a private household wishing to protect a single PC you almost certainly are – then download and install the free package. If you are not eligible to use the free version – you have more than one PC or your PC is attached to a network – you should visit **www.grisoft.com** and check on the licensing of their paid-for products and trial versions. You can also download a reference guide and an installation guide from their site.

To find out more about AVG Free Edition and AVG Trial Versions visit **http://free.grisoft.com**.

Installing the anti-virus package – whether AVG or other – is no different from installing any other piece of software on your system. Make sure that you have sufficient rights – you'll need Administrator rights – and click on the installer file icon to start the process. Follow the on-screen instructions until the installer has finished running – you may have to reboot the system at some point. The example which follows is of AVG Free edition – illustrations by courtesy of Grisoft sro, Czech Republic.

1   The AVG installer has the company logo on its icon – see Figure 16.01 – click on this to start the installation process.

Figure 16.01

2   You will see a Welcome screen – read the instructions and copyright statement – then click **Next** if you wish to install the product.

3   You will be presented with a licence agreement. Read this, and click **Accept**, then at the next screen click **Accept** again. The AVG installer will now check your system. When this is done you must select your installation type.

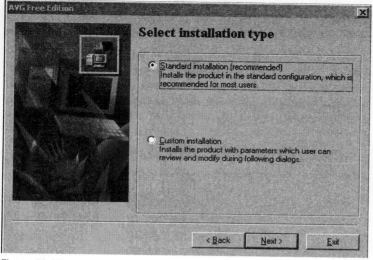

Figure 16.02

4   The default is a Standard Installation. Accept this and click **Next**. Select **Next** again at the Confirmation screen.

5   Click **Finish** to start the final phase of the installer. This may take a couple of minutes and at the end of it you will see an Installation complete! message. Click **OK** to end.

6   The next phase is a post-install setup which launches itself automatically. You will probably receive a warning that the anti-virus database is out of date. That's because you haven't

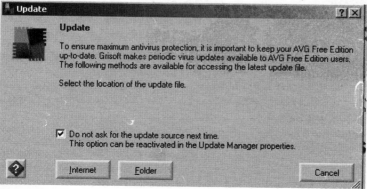

Figure 16.03

updated it yet! Click **Next** and check for updates – connect to the Internet and select the *Internet* option. AVG will check for updates and if there are any available you will be prompted to download them. Note that you can check the box – as in Figure 16.03 – so that future updates will be downloaded from the Internet without prompting.

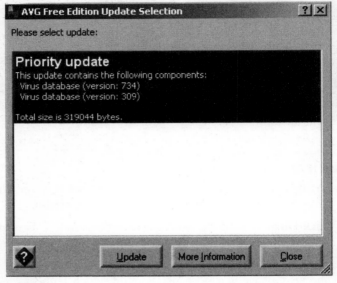

Figure 16.04

7 Click **Update** to download the latest virus definition files. AVG will install any available ones. It may be useful to check again for updates – there may be more than one – until you are informed that there are no further updates available.

8 You will be prompted to make a Rescue Disk – have a spare formatted floppy available if you want to do this – or you can just click **Next**. Either way, all you need to do from here onwards is to accept the default values suggested by selecting **Next** at each screen until you have finished.

9 With the installation finished and the definition files updated, the AVG Test Center will open (Figure 16.05).

10 Click **Scan Computer** to start a full system scan. This may take several minutes. With luck, you will receive an 'all clear'

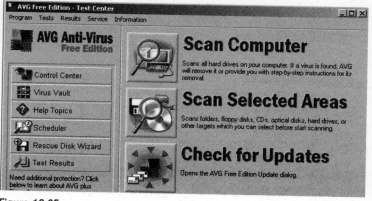

Figure 16.05

message at the end of the scan, in which case you should now configure the package to automatically check for updates from time to time and to do periodic system scans.

11 If a virus is detected, then go to section 16.5, *How to deal with a virus infection*.

Scheduling updates and scans

Whatever anti-virus package you have installed, you need to consider how to organize regular updates and system scans that fit in with your pattern of PC use and your type of Internet connection. Again, this is illustrated by reference to AVG Free, though similar procedures should be available in any other anti-virus package that you may choose.

If you have an always-on broadband connection you can schedule updates for times when you won't be actually working on the PC, with a system scan scheduled to run after any update.

1 To schedule updates and tests click **Scheduler**, highlight the entry for **Update Plan**, then click **Edit Scheduler** and set a time to check for updates.

Here, the update check will be made between 02.00 and 03.59 in the morning, with a fall-back provision so that if the PC isn't connected a check will be run when it is next online.

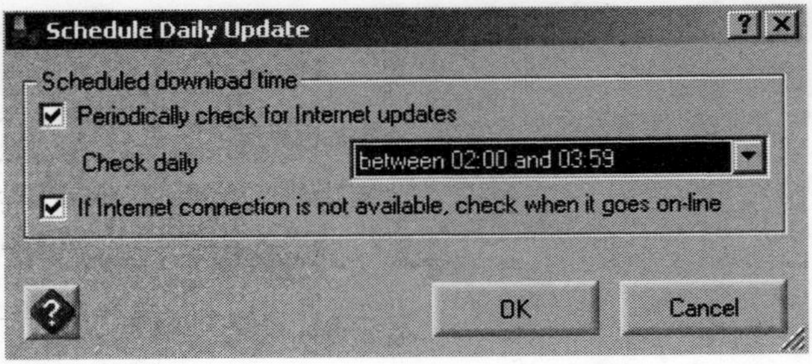

Schedule Daily Update ? X

Scheduled download time
☑ Periodically check for Internet updates
Check daily   between 02:00 and 03:59 ▼
☑ If Internet connection is not available, check when it goes on-line

❓   OK   Cancel

Figure 16.06

2 Having set up the regular update, return to the Scheduler, highlight **Test Plan**, then click **Edit Scheduler**. Set this for (say) 4a.m. so that the update check has been done and the full system scan will run afterwards but before you start work on your PC next day.

These settings will also work if you are using a dialup connection or you are not always connected to the Internet, though they will run at start-up time and you may find this a little inconvenient. However, these are necessary basic precautions against virus attack and a little inconvenience is a small price to pay for security.

16.3 Spyware and ad-ware

Spyware and ad-ware have become an increasing problem for many users in recent years. These packages may be relatively harmless – cookies that track your surfing habits so that you can be sent targeted advertising – or they may be attempts at identity theft, aimed at stealing your name, passwords, bank details, etc. Then there are grey areas – software which is 'advertising supported' – i.e. you agree to view targeted advertising as the price of using 'free' software. Real free software, like Open Office or Thunderbird, doesn't do this. Some commercial software is quite open about this, displaying a clear licence agreement at install time, but some other ad-ware providers are less honest.

Whatever the exact nature of the ad-ware or spyware, it all takes up resources and slows your system down at best. At worst, it is intrusive, unpleasant and possibly illegal. You should certainly have the right to know what has been installed on your PC and given the tools to remove it if you wish.

A number of spyware and ad-ware products have appeared in recent years in order to meet PC users' concerns. One of these – Windows Defender – is supplied with Vista. It is also available as a free download for users of XP Home and XP Professional.

Windows Defender in XP

Note, you must have XP Service Pack 2 installed to install Windows Defender.

1 Visit the Microsoft website and follow the link to Windows Defender. At the time of writing, this software is still under development – classified by Microsoft as *Beta 2*.

2 You will need to validate your copy of Windows – click on **Continue** as shown in Figure 16.07.

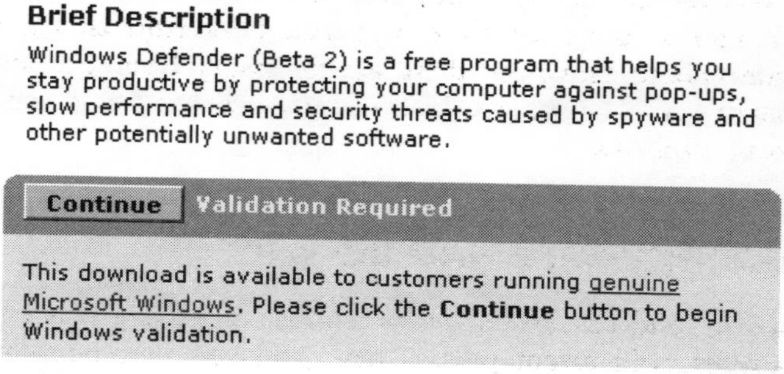

Brief Description

Windows Defender (Beta 2) is a free program that helps you stay productive by protecting your computer against pop-ups, slow performance and security threats caused by spyware and other potentially unwanted software.

Continue Validation Required

This download is available to customers running genuine Microsoft Windows. Please click the **Continue** button to begin Windows validation.

Figure 16.07

3 This may require you to download and install a plug-in to validate your copy of Windows. If this is necessary, click the **Download plug in** button. This will initiate the download of a small program to your PC. Click the program icon to install this then return to the Microsoft site.

4 Click **Continue**. You will be taken to a screen with another **Continue** button which will start the validation (Figure 16.08).

5 You can now download Defender. This is a 6.4Mb file which will take a couple of minutes on a broadband connection – or around 15 minutes over a dialup line. You can run this

Genuine Windows Validation

Thank you for taking part in genuine Windows validation. Validating will enable you to receive your download now and quickly access other downloads and additional benefits in the future. To complete the validation process, we need you to provide some additional information.

Please click **Continue** to complete the validation process.

> Continue

Figure 16.08

program from the Microsoft site, or download it and run it from your own PC. Either way, you will end up with an installed copy of Windows Defender.

6   The installer will present you with a Welcome screen where you can choose the program settings that you wish to use.

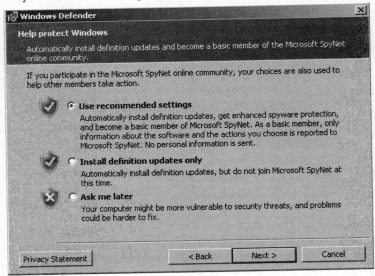

Figure 16.09

7   Select an option, then click **Next**. From here on, you may safely accept the default values until the installer is finished.

8   The installer will offer to check for updates and run a quick scan. Clear the box if you don't want to do this. Click **Finish**.

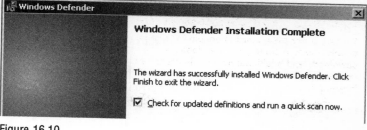

Figure 16.10

9 If you run the update, **Defender** will access the Internet, download any available update files, then scan your system.

10 The default installation of Windows Defender will place an icon in XP's **All Programs** menu and a launcher in the notification area. Start Defender from either of these to customize your setup. If you see a warning that the definitions file hasn't been updated for a while, do it now! Click **Check for Updates** to start a manual update. When this is done, you can configure automatic updates for the future.

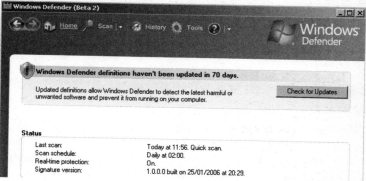

Figure 16.11

11 The toolbar has five items. **Home** takes you back to this opening screen, **Scan** starts a scan of your system. **History** will be empty at this point because you have only just installed it and **Help** – indicated by a question mark – will take you to a useful online manual. The most important item in the menu bar is **Tools** – this is where you configure Defender to check daily for updates, to download new components and definitions and to run a scan after doing so.

12 Open the Tools menu and select General Settings to reach the screen shown in Figure 16.12. Use the drop-down lists to set the frequency and time of updates, to start a scan after checking for updates and the default action to take for each level of threat. Having made your selections, click **Save** so that these options will be made permanent.

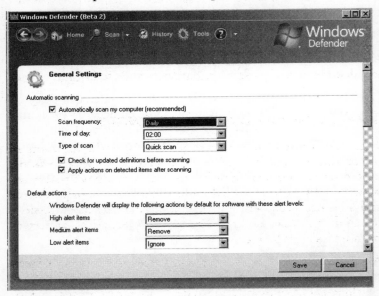

Figure 16.12

There are more options which allow you to fine-tune Windows Defender, but they are beyond the scope of this book. As with so many things in computing, once you have the basics – experiment and read the manual, then, perhaps, experiment again!

Other spyware and ad-ware detection packages

Windows Defender is not the only tool available for spyware and ad-ware detection and removal. There are several other packages – such as Lavasoft's AdAware or Spybot Search and Destroy which can be downloaded free for personal use.

Phishing filter in Internet Explorer 7

Phishing (pronounced 'fishing') is the increasingly common practice of sending emails which appear to come from a reputable source such as your bank, asking you to confirm contact details, login information or even passwords. The best way to avoid trouble is simply to delete any suspicious emails. However, as an extra layer of precaution, Internet Explorer version 7 gives you the opportunity to set up a Phishing filter. IE7 ships with Vista and a free download is available for XP users. If you are running XP and you haven't already done so, download this free upgrade, install it and follow the instructions to activate the Phishing filter.

16.4 Parental control software

There is no censorship on the World Wide Web – no one owns it or controls it – and for the most part that is beneficial to all of us. However, it does mean that there are some pretty unpleasant websites varying from the salacious to the downright perverted and no matter what we may think about freedom of expression for adults most people agree that children should be protected from undesirable web content.

As with spyware and ad-ware, public perception of the problems of pornography, violence or racism on the Net, has led to the development of software tools to deal with the problems, and to restrict access to sites which you regard as unsuitable. There are a number of commercial products which give you control over Internet access and Vista comes bundled with its own parental control software.

The parental controls in Vista are set up though the Control Panel applet *Windows Parental Control*. Use of this is outlined towards the end of Chapter 3, *Control Panel*. Parental control software has been available as a third-party add-on for several years. These tend to be reasonably priced rather than free. Two of the best known of these are Net Nanny and Cyber Sentinel. These can be bought on disk from some retail outlets or downloaded from the Internet. They are similar in operation to the Vista parental control software.

16.5 How to deal with a virus infection

If you think that you have a virus infection, the first thing to do is to scan your system with an up-to-date virus scanner. If you don't have a scanner, or it is out of date, then install one and obtain any necessary updates for it before you do anything else.

If your system won't boot at all, or only boots sporadically, then you should check that it isn't a hardware problem caused by a defective power supply unit. If the PSU is okay, then you may have a boot sector virus. Fixing this is relatively easy. If you have a start-up disk from an old Windows 98 or Me system then you can boot to it and from the command prompt, issue the command FDISK /MBR – even though this is the 'wrong' Windows version it will replace the Master Boot Record on the target hard disk. It is absolutely essential that this boot floppy is write-protected. If it is not then it will become infected with the virus that you are trying to remove from the hard disk. To make sure that the floppy is write-protected, check that you can see daylight through both of the holes in the floppy disk's casing.

1   If you don't have a start-up disk, you can achieve the same outcome by booting your PC with an installation CD or DVD – this probably won't work with a manufacturer's restore disk. The installation CD will run, loading drivers and so forth, until it reaches a screen with the choices:

    ◆ Set up Windows – press [Enter].

    ◆ Repair an installation of Windows – press [R].

    ◆ Quit Set up – press [F3].

2   Press [R]. You will be presented with a list of installations. For most users this will be a list with one element labelled:

    1. C:\WINDOWS

3   Pressing [Enter] will cancel the repair. Press [1], then [Enter] to start the Recovery Console. If you set an Administrator password at install time you will need to enter it.

4   At the Recovery Console, run the utility FIXMBR by entering this at the command prompt. You will be asked if you are sure you want to do this – press [Y] and [Enter].

5 After FIXMBR has run, type EXIT and press [Enter] to reboot the machine. Don't forget to remove the installation disk from the drive and store it somewhere safe.

Whichever of the techniques you have used – FDISK /MBR or FIXMBR – you will now have a clean, new Master Boot Record on your hard disk, but the job isn't finished yet!

Just because you have fixed the boot sector virus that was the immediate problem it doesn't mean to say that there aren't other copies or other viruses elsewhere on your hard disk or floppies. There are three things that you need to check thoroughly:

◆ Your hard disk(s) – do a full scan with an up-to-date virus scanner. It is a good idea to disable System Restore while scanning so that the scanner can search and destroy anything hiding in the protected system area. You will lose any system restore points, but it's a price worth paying for an effective full scan. Don't forget to turn it on when you have finished!

◆ Floppy disks – scan and mark with a pen or sticky label every floppy disk that you have. Make sure you check any disks that belong to other family members.

◆ Scan backups and archives – you may have backed up the virus before you realized it was present.

Some viruses require you to download a specific cleanup program. Most of the major anti-virus companies maintain a list of current 'top threats' on their websites and make cleanup programs available for particular known pests.

Summary

This chapter has looked at some of the common threats from the Internet and outlined the measures necessary to keep your system safe. Where viruses and spyware are concerned the real answer is vigilance. Be careful about opening attachments in emails, particularly from people you don't know; only download drivers and utilities from known reputable sites; above all keep your anti-virus and spyware updated. Last week's version of a virus definition file is of limited use – last month's is worse than useless.

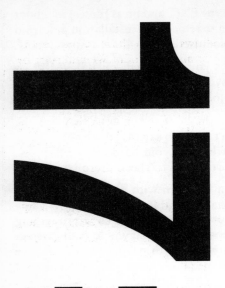

17

home networking

In this chapter you will learn:

- how to set up a small network

- how to share files, printers, an Internet connection and a common file store

17.1 LAN basics

A basic home network that allows you to share resources and files is straightforward to set up and maintain. We will start by setting up a Local Area Network (LAN) of just two PCs. Once we have them working we will then look at how to extend the network to include additional machines.

Before we start on the practicalities, however, we need to look at some network basics. Some of this may look a bit odd at first sight, but it's not really too difficult.

IP address

Every PC on your home network needs an Internet Protocol (IP) address. This is a set of numbers which act like a phone number for each PC. A typical private IP address might look like this: 192.168.0.1.

Subnet mask

The standard subnet masks for home networking are either 255.255.0.0 (Class 'B') or 2555.255.255.0 (Class 'C') – Windows will allocate these for you when you set up your network.

NetBIOS name

The name that you give to the PC. It must be 15 characters or less in length and can't contain spaces or special characters like @ or & or $.

You can't have duplicate names on the same network. In this chapter we will be using the names STEINBECK and ASIMOV – both of which comply with these rules.

Your network keeps track of the names and IP addresses just as a telephone directory matches names and phone numbers.

Workgroup

In order to see each other, your PCs have to be in the same workgroup. In this chapter we will use the name HAVEN for our workgroup.

17.2 Physical connections

Obviously there has to be some form of physical connection between the PCs that are part of a network – even wireless is considered to be a physical connection.

Most modern PCs have an Ethernet LAN port at the back. These are roughly rectangular in section and are somewhere between a phone plug and a modem plug in size. You will need a network cable to connect your PCs, so an easy way to tell which is the Ethernet port is to try the cable. If the cable – which uses a connector called an RJ-45 – fits, then it is an Ethernet port.

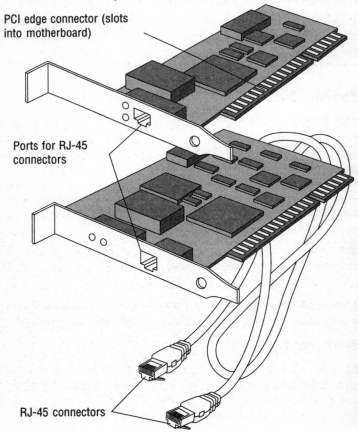

PCI edge connector (slots into motherboard)

Ports for RJ-45 connectors

RJ-45 connectors

Figure 17.01 A basic networking starter kit

If you don't have an Ethernet port, you will need a Network Interface Card (NIC) for each of the PCs . You will also need a crossover cable to connect a pair of machines back-to-back as in the example below. This is a special type of cable designed for use with just two PCs. You may be able to buy a network starter kit which will contain a crossover cable and two network cards.

Fitting the cards

Your network cards will fit in one of the standard PCI expansion slots inside your PC. To do this, power down, remove the cover and fit the new card. Power up again. If the card plugs and plays out of the box, fine. Otherwise, you will have to provide software drivers from the card manufacturer's CD when prompted by Windows. If you are in doubt about how to do this, turn back to Chapters 7 and 8 and review the precautions and procedures.

Joining the PCs with the crossover cable

With both PCs powered up, insert the RJ-45 plug at each end of the cable into the Ethernet port on the back of each machine. You will now need to wait for a minute or so while the PCs find each other. Then it's time to test your connection. To do this, the easiest way is to start a command prompt and to use the PING command. In this example we will PING the PC called ASIMOV from the PC called STEINBECK. The results will look like this:

```
Command Prompt

Microsoft Windows XP [Version 5.1.2600]
(C) Copyright 1985-2001 Microsoft Corp.

C:\Documents and Settings\Isaac>PING ASIMOV

Pinging ASIMOV [169.254.187.195] with 32 bytes of data:

Reply from 169.254.187.195: bytes=32 time=1ms TTL=128
Reply from 169.254.187.195: bytes=32 time<1ms TTL=128
Reply from 169.254.187.195: bytes=32 time<1ms TTL=128
Reply from 169.254.187.195: bytes=32 time<1ms TTL=128

Ping statistics for 169.254.187.195:
    Packets: Sent = 4, Received = 4, Lost = 0 (0% loss),
Approximate round trip times in milli-seconds:
    Minimum = 0ms, Maximum = 1ms, Average = 0ms

C:\Documents and Settings\Isaac>
```

Figure 17.02

As an alternative, in XP click **My Network Places** then **View Workgroup Computers**. In Vista click **Start** then **Networks** – you will see something like Figure 17.03.

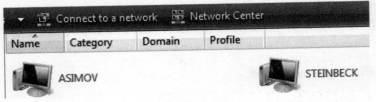

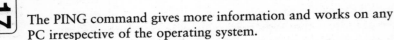

Figure 17.03

The PING command gives more information and works on any PC irrespective of the operating system.

If you are having problems at this stage, check that the cable is secure at both ends and that the PCs are in the same workgroup. The default is WORKGROUP so if you changed this, check that it is the same on both PCs. Right-click on My Computer, select **Properties** from the menu, then choose the **Computer Name** tab.

Another problem may be your firewall settings. While you are experimenting with setting up your home network and you are not connected to the Internet you can turn off the firewall on all PCs. When your network is running, you will need to enable the firewall only on the PC that connects directly to the Internet.

17.3 Setting up user accounts

If you are used to working with a standalone PC you may have it set up to log you in automatically when you turn on. Even if you have more than one user on your family PC, you may not have password-protected accounts. This can cause problems with networking, so add a password to any existing accounts or create password-protected accounts for your users.

Create the same accounts on the other PC. To keep things simple, use the same passwords on each of the PCs on your network. If you need to create new accounts, follow the procedures shown in section 3.8, *User Accounts*. To add a password, run the User Accounts applet. Click on the user's name and select the *Create Password* option, and follow the prompts.

17.4 Sharing files in XP

Sharing files in Windows XP is very easy because Windows uses a default Simple File Sharing system.

If users want to make their My Documents folders available to others on the network, all they have to do is to right-click on My Documents and select **Properties** from the context menu. The **Sharing** tab gives the option to share the files on the network.

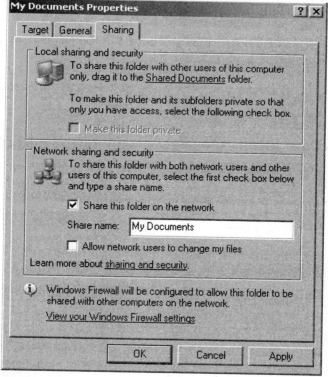

Figure 17.04

With the file-sharing regime set up as in Figure 17.04, other users will be able to read, but not modify the shared files. Checking the **Allow network users to change my files** will give them complete access. You need to do this if they are to be allowed to save files to this folder.

Note: when you set up file sharing like this you may receive a warning from Windows about the risks. If this happens, choose the option to set up file sharing without using the Wizard.

To check that the share is working, log on to the other PC and navigate to the newly shared folder through *My Network Places*. The newly shared folder should appear as in Figure 17.05.

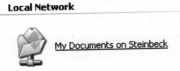

Figure 17.05

17.5 Sharing files in Vista

Setting up file sharing in Vista is slightly different. The owner right-clicks on the icon of the file (or folder) to be shared and selects **Share** from the menu. This dialog box appears.

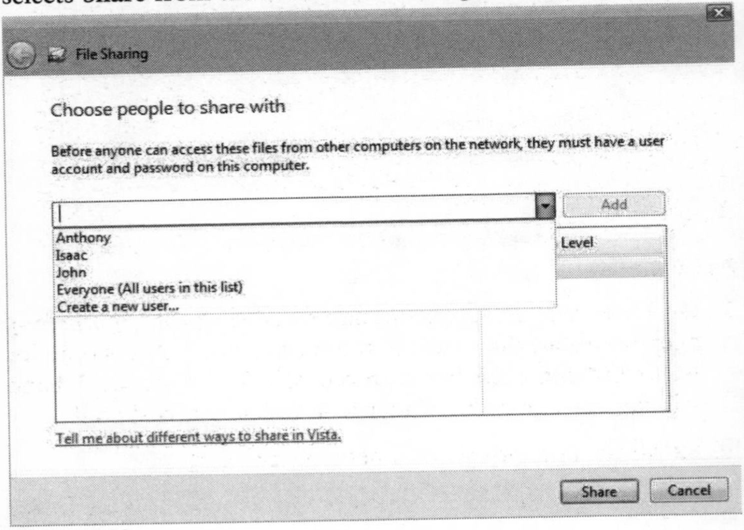

Figure 17.06

To grant sharing rights, the owner of the folder can select names from the drop-down list, or select **Everyone** or, if they have sufficient administrative rights, they can create a new user. The owner of the folder clicks **Share** and the folder will be available over the network.

17.6 Sharing a printer in XP

To make a printer available on the network, we have to do two things:

◆ Set up a share on the printer where it is connected.

◆ Install it on the other PCs in the network.

To set up the share on the local printer:

1 Open the Printers and Faxes folder from the Start menu, right-click on the printer icon and select **Properties** from the menu.

2 On the **Sharing** tab, select the *Share this Printer* option.

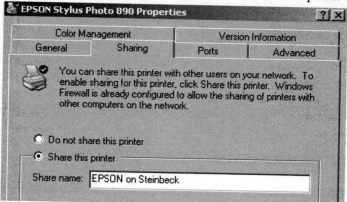

Figure 17.07

3 Give the share a meaningful name and click **OK**. Ignore any warning about the length of the share name – this is only for backward compatibility with old MS-DOS systems. A hand will appear under the printer icon to show it is shared.

To install the new printer as a network printer:

1 Log on to the other PC. Open the Printers and Faxes folder and select **Add a Printer**.

2 Step through the wizard, making sure that you select **Install a network printer** at the appropriate point. You will be given the option to browse for a printer as part of the setup routine – this can sometimes take a minute or two so be patient. Eventually you will see something like Figure 17.08.

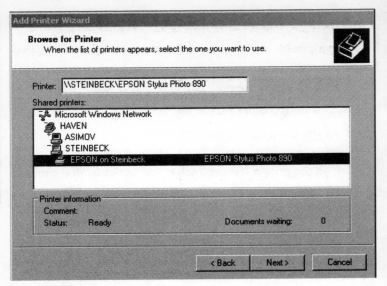

Figure 17.08

3 Highlight the printer you wish to install and click **Next**. You will receive a warning about installing drivers – click **Yes** to continue. Windows will install the drivers and you will be given the option to make this the default printer for this PC. Make your choice, click **Next**, then click **Finish**.

4 Finally, right-click the new printer icon, and select **Properties** then click the **Print Test Page** button.

17.7 Sharing a printer in Vista

Enabling printer sharing on the Vista PC is even easier! Just navigate to **Control Panel > Hardware and Sound > Printers** and right-click on the installed printer. Select **Sharing** from the context menu. You will see a dialog box like the one in Figure 17.09.

Select the **Share this printer** radio button and change the default name of the share if you want to. At this point you can also install additional drivers for use by PCs running a different Windows version – useful if you want to print from XP machines on your network. When you have made your selections, click **OK** to save your preferences.

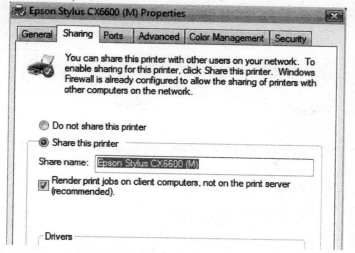

Figure 17.09 Sharing a printer on a Vista PC

17.8 Sharing an Internet connection

There are two ways of doing this: connect through a standalone modem/router, or connect through a shared modem attached to a single PC with the connection shared by other PCs on your home network. The basics of setting up these connections are covered in Chapter 15, *The Internet and email*. Sharing the connections is the topic which we will consider here.

Connecting through a router

If you are using a combined ADSL modem/router then connection is all but automatic for any PC that you attach to your home network. Vista, in particular, will auto-detect most ADSL modems/routers and run a Wizard.

If, after you have connected a second PC to your network, you can't 'see' the Internet from it, check that you have a working connection on the first machine. If you are still having problems after that, check that the new PC is set up to obtain an IP address automatically (this is the default for Windows systems) by checking the properties of your LAN connection. Here's how.

1 Open the Control Panel and select **Network Connections** then right-click on the icon for your LAN connection and select **Properties**. Select *Internet Protocol (TCP/IP)* from the list.

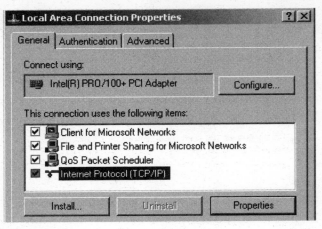

Figure 17.10

2 Click **Properties**. The screen should now look like this.

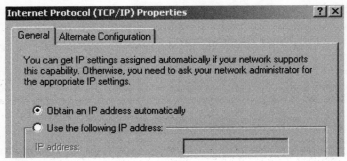

Figure 17.11

3 If necessary, change the setting to **Obtain an IP address automatically** and click **OK** to save your changes.

4 If you are still having problems, it may be that your PC is looking for a previous modem or dialup connection. In the Control Panel, run **Internet Options** and open the **Connections** tab (Figure 17.12).

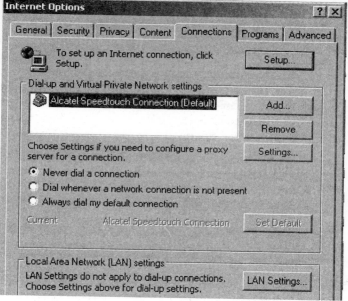

Figure 17.12

5 If a modem connection is present, and you are no longer using it, remove it by clicking **Remove**, or leave it but select **Never dial a connection**.

6 Now make sure that you connect through your network. To do this, click **LAN Settings**, tick the *Automatically detect settings* box and click **OK** to confirm this. This will force your PC to connect to the Internet through your router.

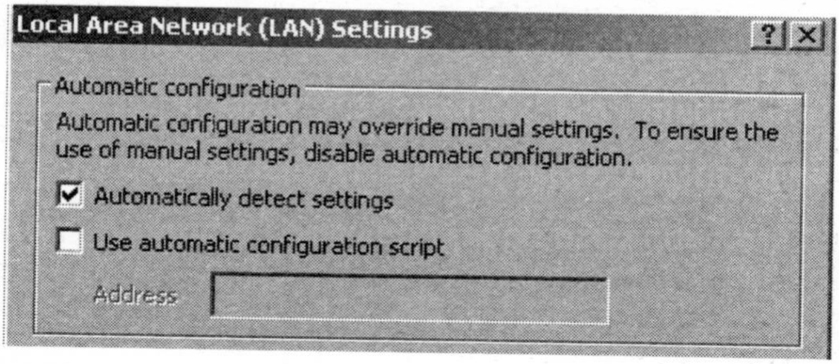

Figure 17.13

Sharing a modem connection

This is a bit more fiddly to set up than connecting through a router, but it's not particularly difficult. Running the Internet Connection Wizard configures the PC with the modem attached to it as a router through which other PCs on your network connect to the Internet. Before running the Wizard, make sure that you have a modem – dial-up or broadband – connected and working (refer back to Chapter 15 if you need to). You will also need a blank formatted floppy disk to use with the Wizard.

1 In the Control Panel click the **Network Setup Wizard**. If you have a working network, all you need to do is to step through the Wizard making appropriate choices. Most of the defaults are sensible, but there are a couple of points to watch out for.

2 When you are asked to select a connection method, make sure that you select *This computer connects directly to the Internet* if this is the PC which has the modem attached to it.

3 You need to choose the modem to use for the shared connection – Windows doesn't always 'guess' this properly. Highlight the appropriate connection and click **Next**.

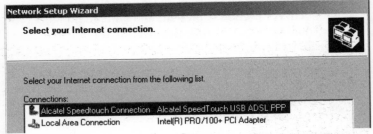

Figure 17.14

4 You have the opportunity to change the PC's name – do this only if it is a requirement by your ISP. Click **Next**.

5 The setup Wizard always defaults to MSHOME as the workgroup name, so you need to enter your chosen name here. Click **Next**.

6 You can choose whether or not you wish to enable file and printer sharing – you probably do. Make your choice and click **Next**.

7 You will be shown a summary screen of your settings. You can go back and change them or click **Next** to accept them. Once this is done the Wizard will take a minute or two to configure your system.

8 The final step is to create a Network Setup disk which you can use to configure other PCs on your network. Insert a floppy in the A: drive and click **Next**. (You can use any removable drive such as a USB 'pen' drive if you like.) Follow the instructions to create the disk. Remove it from the drive.

9 Check your modem and, if you want to, allow all users of the system to use it, then connect to make sure that it is working.

17.9 Setting up the other PCs

Having made the Network Setup disk, the next task is to run it on the other PCs that you want to share the connection with.

1 Put the disk in the drive of the other machine. Click on My Computer, then click on the icon for the floppy drive. It contains a single file called NTSETUP. Click on this to run it.

2 You will see a Welcome screen – click **Yes** to start the Wizard. It will present you with the options shown here.

Network Setup Wizard

Welcome to the Network Setup Wizard

This wizard will help you set up this computer to run on your network. With a network you can:

• Share an Internet connection
• Set up Windows Firewall
• Share files and folders
• Share a printer

Figure 17.15

3 Click **Next** to continue. Read the checklist on screen and make sure that everything is connected and that you are connected to the Internet. Click **Next**.

4 Choose the option *This computer connects to the Internet through a residential gateway or another computer on my network*, then click **Next**.

5 At the next screen you can confirm the PC's name and/or add a description – click **Next**.

6 Even though you changed the workgroup name when making the Network Setup disk the workgroup will have reverted to the default MSHOME. Change this so that this PC is a member of the same workgroup as the one where you installed the modem – otherwise it won't work. Click **Next**.

7 You will be given the opportunity (again) to enable or disable file and print sharing. Make your choice and click **Next**. The next screen gives you a review of your settings. Change or confirm them and when you are satisfied, click **Next**.

8 After a minute or two you will be given the choice to make a Network Setup Disk. You already have one, so select the *Use the Network Setup Disk I already have* and click **Next**.

9 The next screen tells you to repeat these steps on any other computer that you want to share the Internet connection with. Click **Next**, then **Finish**.

10 Run your Internet browser to test the connection, then close the browser.

11 As a final test, disconnect from the Internet on the PC that has the modem, then go back to the one where you have set up the share and launch the browser again. Provided you set up the modem to allow any user to connect you should see the Internet after a couple of seconds. If you have more PCs on your network, you can run the Network Setup disk on each of them to give them Internet access. The only restriction on this shared access is, of course, that the PC with the modem must be running for the others to connect through it.

Connection sharing in Vista

The mechanics of sharing a connection in Vista are similar to those in XP, but the Network Setup Wizard is even easier to use. Navigate to: **Control Panel > Network Center > Set Up a Connection**. Click **Set up a Network** to start the Network Connection Wizard, then follow the on-screen prompts.

17.10 Sharing a common file store

Even on a small home network it is possible to use a single PC as a central file store, or *file server*. The advantage of this arrangement is mainly that of easy backup: if all user data is kept in one area then backing up everyone's files can be done in a single operation. The main disadvantages of this approach are that the file server PC has to be on all the time, and that all users need to have an account on that PC as well as on the one that they use for their work. Maintaining these user accounts for a small number of people is not too difficult. However, if you have a lot of users, or, members of the workgroup change frequently, then it rapidly becomes more trouble than it is worth. Also, the XP Home version of Windows limits the number of simultaneous network connections to five. A larger network will need a client/server setup which is beyond the scope of this book.

Creating the shared file store (XP)

Once you have nominated one of your PCs as the always-on file server, the first thing to do is to create a folder for everyone's files and set up a share on it. To do this, navigate through My Computer to the icon for drive C:. You may receive a warning that the files on C: are hidden – if this happens select the option to make them visible. You should see something like Figure 17.16. The left pane shows the tools available to you; the right pane shows the folders on the C: drive.

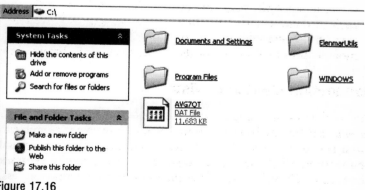

Figure 17.16

1 Right-click on an empty space in the right pane and select **New** from the context menu.

2 Create a **New Folder**.

3 Right-click on the New Folder and rename it *User-Data* (or any other descriptive name).

4 Right-click on the new *User-Data* folder and select **Sharing and Security** from the context menu. Check the boxes to **Share this folder on the network** and **Allow network users to change my files**.

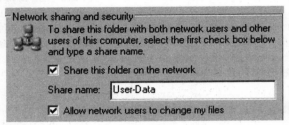

Figure 17.17

The *User-Data* folder will now appear with a hand under it, indicating that it is a shared resource on your network.

5 Go into the *User-Data* folder, then right-click on an empty area and create a folder each for your users as in Figure 17.18.

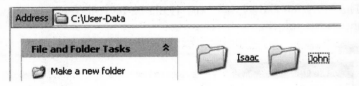

Figure 17.18

Creating the shared file store (Vista)

The process of creating the shared file store in Vista is similar to that outlined for XP. Create a shared storage area on a local hard drive (typically C:) and make it available on the network by granting permissions to the users that you want to have access. See *Sharing files in Vista* on page 244, and Figure 17.06.

Whether you have used an XP machine or a Vista machine for your shared file store, the next step is to relocate each user's data so that it is held in the shared area and new items will automatically be saved there. This is remarkably easy to do.

Relocating My Documents

By default, each user's *My Documents* folder is kept in C:\Documents and Settings*username*\\My Documents (XP) or C:\Users*username*\\Documents (Vista). These locations can be changed as follows:

1 Right-click on *(My)Documents* and select **Properties**. This will show the location of the files belonging to the current user. Click **Move...**

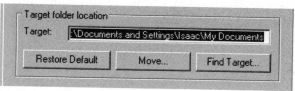

Figure 17.19

2 Navigate to the user's new folder and click **OK**.

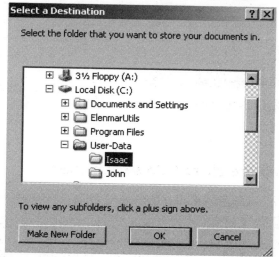

Figure 17.20

3 Windows will show you the new location. If it is correct, click **Apply**.

4 You will now be asked if you want Windows to move that user's files to the new folder. Click **Yes** if you do.

5 Repeat 1–4 for each user on the PC with the shared file store.

6 Repeat this for each user on each of the other PCs, this time setting a network path to the shared folder (see Figure 17.21).

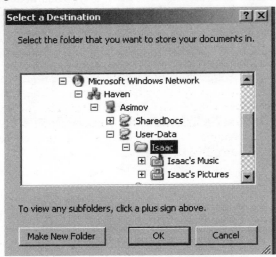

Figure 17.21

A note on security

The shared file store that we have examined here makes it easy – too easy perhaps – to share files. As things stand, anyone can see or modify anyone else's files if they take the trouble to navigate to them across the network through My Network Places. This is because we are using the default Simple File Sharing of a standard Windows home user setup. This makes things easy to set up at the cost of virtually no security between user accounts.

A higher level of security can be achieved by using NTFS file permissions even on a peer-to-peer network of this type. Full security can be implemented on a domain-based client/server network.

These topics are beyond this book, but if you are interested in developing a bigger and better secured network, you could look at *Teach Yourself PC Networking for Small Businesses*. This addresses the needs of the small business and the more ambitious home user.

17.11 Adding to your network

Once you have a basic two-PC network in place and running it is easy to add further nodes to your network. In order to do this you will need a different cable type – a straight-through Ethernet cable instead of a crossover – and a workgroup switch or hub.

A switch is more efficient than a hub, though the difference in performance is not critical for a home network. Whether switch or hub, you have a box with standard Ethernet ports which provides a central cabling nexus for your network. The hub or switch needs a source of mains power – usually a transformer supplied by the manufacturer.

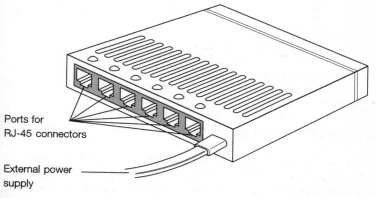

Ports for
RJ-45 connectors

External power
supply

Figure 17.22

To connect your PCs to the hub or switch you will need a straight-through Ethernet cable for each of them. This connects to the Ethernet port on the back of the PC and to one of the ports on the hub/switch. As soon as it is connected you should see one of the lights on the Ethernet card on the PC begin to blink, indicating network activity. The light over (or next to) the port on the switch will show similar signs of life when connected.

From this point onwards, setting up and maintaining your home network is the same as the two-PC example that we used in the earlier part of the chapter. All of the rules concerning IP addresses, user accounts, shared resources and so forth, apply. The only problems which you may encounter will be the complexity of managing a greater number of PCs and user accounts. There are also limits to the number of PCs that you can network simultaneously. Consumer versions of Windows, such as XP Home, generally restrict you to five connections, cannot be joined to a domain, and only have simple file-sharing capabilities.

A note on cables

For the two-PC setup that we looked at in the first part of the chapter, we used a crossover cable. This is a normal Ethernet cable in which send and receive lines have been literally crossed over so that data sent on the send line of one PC is received on the receive line at the other end.

Where you are using a hub or switch, this crossover function is performed by the hub or switch so the cables need to be of the standard straight-through type.

Summary

In this chapter we have looked at the basics of small networks suitable for the home or the micro-business. We have looked at the practicalities of setting up a peer network to share files, a printer and an Internet connection.

If you need a more sophisticated network to accommodate several users and with commercial standards of security, you will need a specialized reference on this type of network such as *Teach Yourself PC Networking for Small Businesses*.

18

wireless networking

In this chapter you will learn:

- how to set up an ad hoc wireless connection
- how to set up a wireless access point
- how to secure your wireless network

18.1 Wireless networking

Wireless networking has become increasingly popular with home users in recent years. It offers a lot of flexibility, particularly if you take a laptop/notebook computer between home and office.

Anything that you can do with a wired network can also be done wirelessly and with a few simple precautions, a wireless network can be as secure as its wired counterpart.

Wireless Networking Standards

There are several wireless networking standards, but only three of these are likely to be of interest to the home user. These are the 802.11b, 802.11g and 802.11n standards.

The 11b standard is the oldest (and slowest) of these so you should, if possible, avoid buying kit which only meets this standard. The 11g standard is faster, but it is backward compatible with the older standard so you can mix equipment on the same network. The latest standard – 11n – is even faster than 11g and is also backward compatible. Whatever you decide to buy, check your existing equipment and make sure that your new kit is backward compatible with it as some users report that there are still some compatibility issues.

Ad hoc Wireless Networks

The simplest type of wireless network is known as an ad hoc network because it has no formal structure. It may consist of a couple of wireless enabled PCs which network when they are in range of one another. This is the easiest way of communicating between a laptop/notebook system – most of which are wireless enabled out of the box – and a desktop machine that has a wireless network connection on board, or installed via an expansion slot on the motherboard.

To set up your wireless network:

1 Open the Control Panel and click on the **Wireless Network Setup** applet. Choose **Set up a new wireless network** and click **Next** (see Figure 18.01).

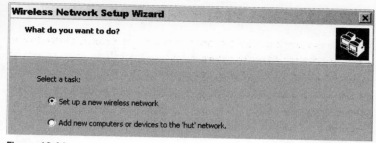

Figure 18.01

2 You will be prompted to supply a name for the new network
   – the Service Set Identifier (SSID). Here the SSID has been set
   to *haven-wifi*. Continue with the Wizard. When you are given
   the choice between USB and Manual setup – choose Manual.

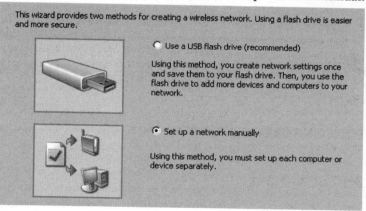

Figure 18.02

3 Click **Next**, then follow the Wizard until it completes. At the
   end, print your network settings and save them. You will
   need them to set up the other end of your network.

4 Repeat the process on the other PC (or laptop) making sure
   that you use the same network settings.

5 With your second machine set up you can connect to your ad
   hoc network. When you click **Connect** you will be shown a
   list of available wireless networks. In the example, there is a
   choice between the new ad hoc connection and an unsecured
   wireless network Jane337. Jane337 is someone else's network

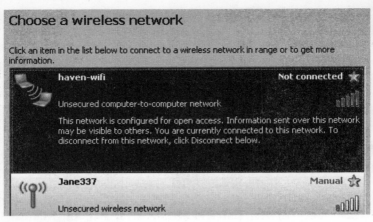

Choose a wireless network

Click an item in the list below to connect to a wireless network in range or to get more information.

| haven-wifi | Not connected ⭐ |
| Unsecured computer-to-computer network |
| This network is configured for open access. Information sent over this network may be visible to others. You are currently connected to this network. To disconnect from this network, click Disconnect below. |

| Jane337 | Manual ⭐ |
| Unsecured wireless network |

Figure 18.03

– possibly a neighbour who has not secured their wireless network. Not only would it be un-neighbourly to connect to this, it would be a breach of the law. To make sure that you are not offering free network access to the neighbours see the Wireless Security section below.

18.2 Wireless Access Points

A Wireless Access Point (WAP) – sometimes known as a 'Base Station' – is the wireless equivalent of a hub or switch on a wired network. It can be attached to a conventional wired network to provide a connection for wireless enabled systems. Although it is beyond the scope of this book, which deals only with PCs running Windows, a Wireless Access Point will enable you to connect any computer, such as a Mac or a PC running a different operating system, so long as it supports wireless networking and the encryption type you have chosen.

Setting up your WAP

The procedures for setting up your Wireless Access Point are broadly similar to setting up an Internet connection through a router – see *Connecting through a router* in Chapter 17. Your WAP will have at least one – probably more – Ethernet ports for connection to a wired LAN. Obviously you will need to read and follow any installation instructions from the manufacturer, but the general procedure is to attach a PC to the LAN port of the WAP and do any necessary configuration tasks.

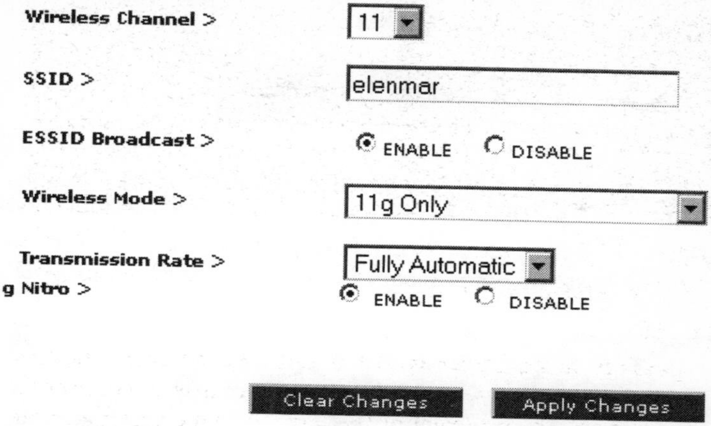

Wireless Channel >	11
SSID >	elenmar
ESSID Broadcast >	⦿ ENABLE ◯ DISABLE
Wireless Mode >	11g Only
Transmission Rate >	Fully Automatic
g Nitro >	⦿ ENABLE ◯ DISABLE

Clear Changes   Apply Changes

Figure 18.04

The **Wireless Channel** is probably best left at the manufacturer's default setting unless there are definite reasons to do otherwise.

The **SSID** field is the name of your wireless network. Set it to whatever you want – it is the name which other PCs will see and use to connect to your wireless network. Note that the SSID is only a name – it does not set up any type of network security.

The **Extended SSID (ESSID) Broadcast** field shown here is set to **Enable**. This means that your access point broadcasts its identity, making it easy to detect and connect from one of your PCs. This function can be disabled if you wish – more on security below.

The **Wireless Mode** field in the figure is set for '11g Only' – this is because this wireless network uses only 11g rated equipment. There are also settings for entirely 11b, for mixed 11b and 11g networks and other, later, standards.

The final field **Transmission Rate**, is probably best left to its default setting of *Fully Automatic*.

18.3 Connecting to your WAP

1 To connect to your WAP from a wireless enabled PC, navigate to **Control Panel > Network Connections** and select the **Wireless Connection** icon.

Figure 18.05

2 The system will display a list of available networks – probably only one (though you may pick up a neighbour's network as well – see section 18.4, *Wireless security*). Unless you have set up some security on your network, your WAP will broadcast its identity and will state that it is insecure.

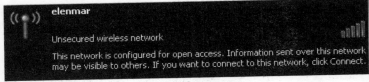

Figure 18.06

3 Clicking **Connect** at this point will result in another security warning as shown in Figure 18.07.

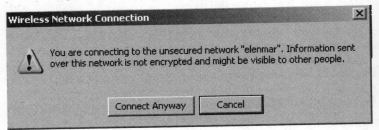

Figure 18.07

4 Click **Connect Anyway** to connect to your network as a test. Bear in mind, that anyone in wireless range can do the same thing until you have put some security measures in place!

ADSL modem/router/WAP

We have already examined ADSL modems, routers and WAPs as separate entities. If you have, say, an ADSL modem, you may want to add a router or a WAP to your system as a separate item. However, there are products from manufacturers, such as Belkin or D-link, which combine these features in a single unit. These are not expensive – typically a two-figure rather than a three-figure price tag – and are generally easy to set up.

(Note: the examples used in this chapter are based on a particular domestic ADSL modem/router. Other makes and models will look different, but will deliver similar functionality.)

18.4 Wireless security

The simplest form of security for the home wireless network is a good choice of name in the SSID field (see Figure 18.04). Choose one as you would a password – something that's easy for you to remember but difficult for someone else to guess. Next, disable the ESSID function. This means that your network will have a name known only to you, and which is not broadcast so will not appear as an available wireless network to anyone else. However, because you know that your wireless network exists and you know its name you can still connect to it. In this example, the SSID has been changed to Fr1day-99 and the ESSID broadcast function has been disabled. Clicking on the Wireless Network icon in Control Panel > Network Connections indicates 'No wireless networks are in range' – this is what you want!

1 To connect to your Fr1day-99 network, right-click on the icon and select **Properties** from the context menu.

2 Choose the **Wireless Networks** tab. Ignore the *View Wireless Networks* button – you have taken steps to ensure that your new network won't be listed here! Instead, click **Add** to open the dialog box shown in Figure 18.08.

3 Type the SSID into the box, change the **Data encryption** field from **WEP** to **Disabled** and save your changes by clicking **OK**. Your new network name will now appear in the list of available networks, though it is still not connected. Click **OK**.

Figure 18.08

4   Return to your wireless network icon and click on it to connect to your unadvertised network. Now that you have set up the connection manually, the network will show up on *your* system and can be configured so that the PC (or laptop) will connect automatically when it is in range. However, to anyone else within range your network is invisible.

For most home users these security steps are probably sufficient. All you really want is to prevent casual or accidental connections by neighbours or anyone else who happens to come in range.

Wireless Protected Access with Pre-Shared Key (WPA/PSK)

This is a means of setting a password on your wireless connection. At the Access Point end of things choose the WPA/PSK option and choose a password – a pre-shared key and note the associated data encryption method – in this case it is TKIP.

WPA >	WPA-PSK (no server)
Encryption technique	**TKIP**
Pre-shared Key (PSK)	✶✶✶✶✶✶✶✶✶✶✶✶

Figure 18.09

1   At the PC end of the connection, right-click on the wireless network connection icon and select **Properties**. Choose the **Wireless Networks** tab and select **Properties**. Enter the PSK (password) in the appropriate field and make sure that the data encryption method matches the one on your WAP.

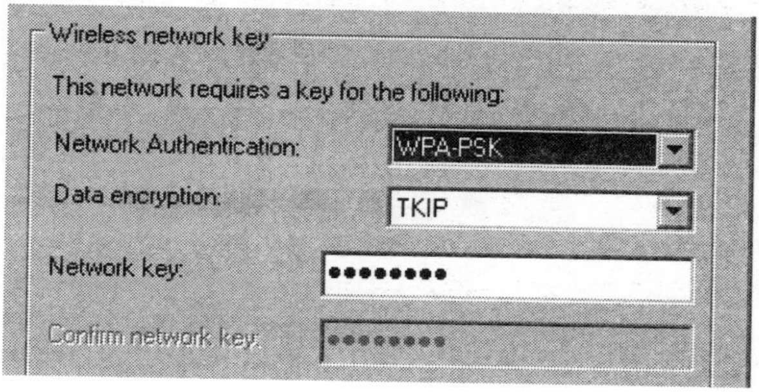

Wireless network key

This network requires a key for the following:

Network Authentication: WPA-PSK

Data encryption: TKIP

Network key: ••••••••

Confirm network key: ••••••••

Figure 18.10

2   Click **OK** to save your changes. Return to your wireless network icon and click on it to connect to your unadvertised and now *secure* network.

Wired Equivalent Privacy (WEP)

Although the security methods we have looked at so far make it difficult for anyone to gain unauthorized access to your wireless network the data is transmitted between PCs in unencrypted form. Anyone with sufficient know-how to access your network (not easy, but possible) could read the data sent between your PCs. As a further level of security it is possible to *encrypt* your data so that it can only be decrypted by someone who has the *encryption key*. The most widely used form of encryption for wireless networks is Wired Equivalent Privacy (WEP).

To set up WEP, you need to access your WAP setup utility, enable WEP and define an encryption key – a word or phrase from which a numeric key will be generated by the system. Clicking the **Generate** button creates the hexadecimal numbers in the figure based on the chosen **Passphrase**. This passphrase becomes, in effect, a password for your network. To connect and to read the data sent across your network it has to be known and implemented at both ends of the connection.

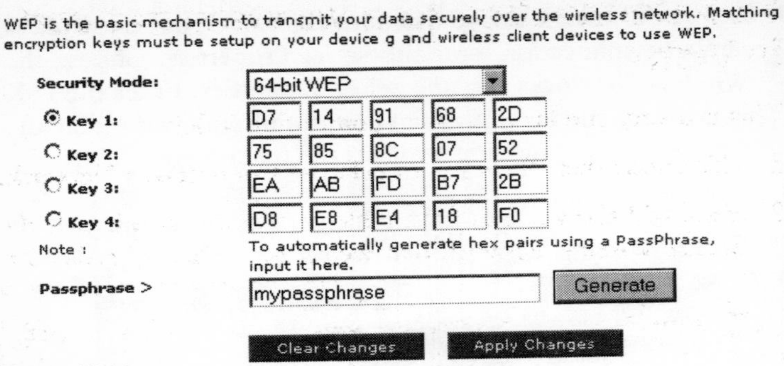

WEP is the basic mechanism to transmit your data securely over the wireless network. Matching encryption keys must be setup on your device g and wireless client devices to use WEP.

Security Mode:	64-bit WEP ▼				
⦿ Key 1:	D7	14	91	68	2D
○ Key 2:	75	85	8C	07	52
○ Key 3:	EA	AB	FD	B7	2B
○ Key 4:	D8	E8	E4	18	F0

Note : To automatically generate hex pairs using a PassPhrase, input it here.

Passphrase > mypassphrase [Generate]

[Clear Changes] [Apply Changes]

Figure 18.11

You then need to configure the connection through Windows. Right-click on your wireless connection and select **Properties**. Choose the **Wireless Networks** tab and click **Add**. Enter the key and click **OK**.

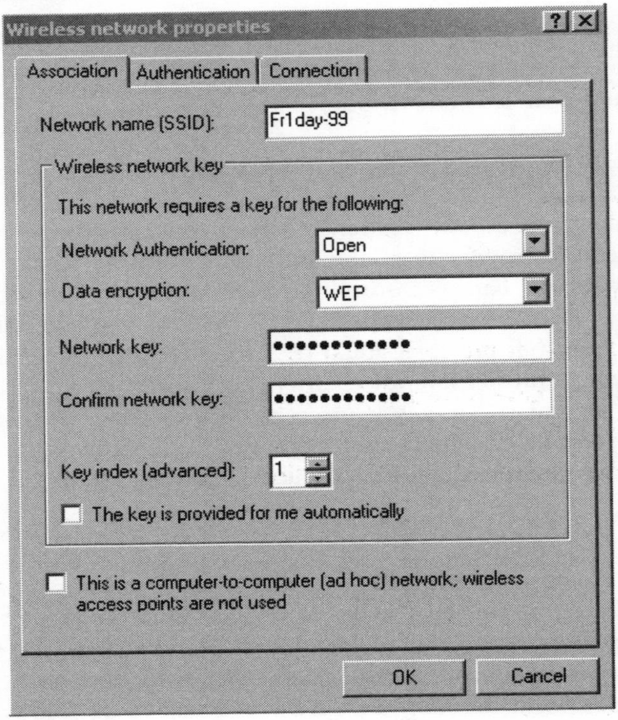

Figure 18.12

18.5 Connecting to a wireless network in Vista

This is a very similar process to connecting in XP.

1 Click **Start** then **Network** and choose **Connect to a Network**.

2 Vista will show a list of available networks – in this case the Secure Wireless network that we set up earlier – Fr1day-99.

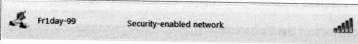

Fr1day-99   Security-enabled network

Figure 18.13

3 Highlight the entry in the list and click on **Connect**.

4 You will be prompted for the security key.

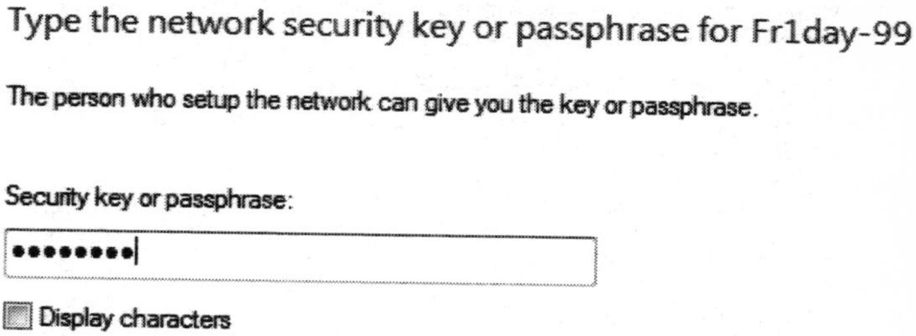

Type the network security key or passphrase for Fr1day-99

The person who setup the network can give you the key or passphrase.

Security key or passphrase:

●●●●●●●●|

☐ Display characters

Figure 18.14

5 Type it in and click on **Next**.

6 If you have provided the correct key, Vista will now connect to your chosen network.

Connected to Fr1day-99 - getting IP address...

Figure 18.15

7 Job done!

Summary

This chapter has examined the basics of wireless networking. We have looked at the simplest of networks – the ad hoc connection which is especially suitable for temporary connections between laptops or a laptop/desktop connection.

We have looked at more structured wireless LANs using a Wireless Access Point (WAP). We have also considered the basics of security which are likely to be sufficient for the needs of the home user.